First Aid Book

Gramercy Publishing Company

New York

This 1985 edition is published by Gramercy Publishing Company,
distributed by Crown Publishers, Inc.,
225 Park Avenue South, New York, New York 10003.

Manufactured in Singapore

Library of Congress Cataloging in Publication Data
First aid book.

   Reprint. Originally published: 1980.
   Bibliography: p.
   Includes index.
   1. First aid in illness and injury.   [DNLM: 1. First
Aid.   2. Wounds and Injuries. WA 292 F527]
RC86.7.F563   1985   616.02′52   84-21256

ISBN: 0-517-466686
h g f e d c b

FOREWORD

Would you know what to do in a medical emergency? Every day accidents occur, some minor, some extremely serious. Often it is a bystander's quick, informed action that saves a life.

The *First Aid Book* is an invaluable tool in any medical emergency, from a grease burn in the kitchen, to dressing wounds, to transporting an injured person safely, to treating people who have swallowed poison. In any medical emergency it is vital not only to take action, but also to be sure that that action does not further endanger the victim in any way. **It is always of primary importance to be sure the victim reaches professional medical care as soon as possible, and the *First Aid Book* is in no way a substitute for calling the paramedics or the family doctor.**

But the *First Aid Book* is extremely useful in that period directly after an accident, before professional medical help arrives. Knowing how to protect an epileptic who has a sudden attack, how to administer "the kiss of life" to a swimmer in distress, how to move—or not move—an accident victim and other such information can make a crucial difference.

The *First Aid Book,* prepared with the assistance of the American Heart Association, the American Red Cross, and many excellent doctors, is a manual that should be in every home.

New York   Anne James
1985

iii

PREFACE

Each year thousands of people are injured or killed in accidents on the job, in the home, and in the community. The purpose of this manual is to provide basic first aid knowledge and skills that will better prepare everyone on and off the job.

This manual is a revision of the Bureau of Mines Instruction Manual, First Aid for the Mineral and Allied Industries. Changes reflected in this book represent current recommended policies and procedures for dealing with emergencies which require first aid.

Special acknowledgement is given to the American Heart Association, the American Red Cross, Mark P. Davis, M.D. of Fairfax Hospital, Virginia, and James C. McClintock of Management Resource, Inc., Monroeville, Pennsylvania, for their assistance in reviewing the material for this book.

CONTENTS

ILLUSTRATIONS

FIRST AID

for the mineral industries

by: Linda H. Byers[1], Layton Revel[2], Wilbur Agee[3], Harry Carter[4]

CHAPTER 1. INTRODUCTION TO FIRST AID

First aid is the immediate care given to a person who is injured or suddenly becomes ill. First aid includes recognizing life-threatening conditions and taking action to keep the injured or ill person alive and in the best possible condition until medical treatment can be obtained.

First aid does not replace the physician. One of the first principles of first aid is to obtain medical assistance in all cases of serious injury. Even minor on-the-job injuries should be promptly reported to appropriate company personnel and, if necessary, examined by a physician.

The principal aims of first aid are as follows:
— To care for life-threatening conditions.

— To minimize further injury and complications.

— To minimize infection.

— To make the victim as comfortable as possible to conserve strength.

— To transport the victim to medical facilities, when necessary, in such a manner as not to complicate the injury or subject the victim to unnecessary discomfort.

First aiders should know how to supply artificial ventilation and circulation, control bleeding, protect injuries from infection and other complications. Arrange for medical assistance and transportation. When first aid is properly administered, the victim's chances of recovery are greatly increased.

[1] Education specialist, Education & Training, Arlington, Virginia
[2] Safety specialist, Education & Training, Dallas, Texas
[3] Training specialist, Education & Training, Arlington, Va. (retired)
[4] Supv. coal mine inspector, Coal Mine Safety & Health, Montgomery, W.Va.

First aiders must be able to take charge of a situation, keep calm while working under pressure, and organize others to do likewise. By demonstrating competence and using well-selected words of encouragement, first aiders should win the confidence of others nearby and do everything possible to reassure the apprehensive victim.

Need for First Aid Training in the Mineral Industries

People should be trained to care properly for injuries to themselves and others at home, at work, or in the community. Because even trivial injuries are potentially serious, everyone should know the proper steps to prevent complications. There is a particular need for first aid training in the mineral industries because medical treatment is often not immediately available at mining sites. In certain cases only a person with first aid training who is nearby can prevent a fatality.

During the first few minutes following an injury, the injured worker has a better chance of receiving proper care if there are a number of employees trained in first aid. All mine employees should be able to give effective assistance until the injured person receives professional medical care.

Experience has shown that training all mining personnel in first aid class where workers, supervisors, and officials meet and learn on a common basis develops a spirit of mutual protection and regard for everyone's well-being.

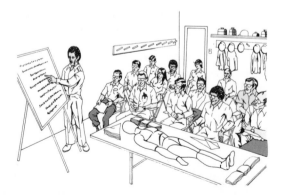

FIGURE 1.01.—First aid class.

Evaluating the Situation

When a person is injured, someone must (1) take charge, (2) administer first aid, and (3) arrange for medical assistance. First aiders should take charge with full recognition of their own limitations and, while caring for life-threatening conditions, direct others briefly and clearly as to exactly what they should do and how to secure assistance.

FIGURE 1.02.—Primary survey.

Primary Survey

Several conditions are considered life-threatening, but three in particular require immediate action:

— Respiratory arrest.

— Circulatory failure.

— Severe bleeding.

Respiratory arrest and/or circulatory failure can set off a chain of events that will lead to death. Severe and uncontrolled bleeding can lead to an irreversible state of shock in which death is inevitable. Death may occur in a very few minutes if an attempt is not

3

made to help the victim in these situations. The first-aider should perform the primary survey to determine the extent of the problem as soon as the victim is reached, and if any of the life-threatening conditions are found, begin first aid procedures without delay.

In checking for adequate breathing, an open airway must be established and maintained. If there are no signs of breathing, artificial ventilation must immediately be given.

If a victim experiences circulatory failure, a person *trained* in cardiopulmonary resuscitation (CPR) should check for a pulse, and, if none is detected, start CPR at once.

A careful and thorough check must be made for any severe bleeding. Serious bleeding must be controlled by proper methods.

In making the primary survey, the first aider must be careful not to move the victim any more than is necessary to support life. Rough handling or any unnecessary movement might cause additional pain and aggravate serious injuries that have not yet been detected.

Secondary Survey

When the life-threatening conditions have been controlled, the secondary survey should begin. The secondary survey is head-to-toe examination to check *carefully* for any additional unseen injuries that can cause serious complications. It is conducted by examining for the following:

- Scalp lacerations and contusions. Without moving the head, check for blood in the hair.

- Skull depressions. Gently feel for possible bone fragments or depressions.

- Loss of fluid or bleeding from the ears and nose, which indicates possible skull fracture and damage to the brain.

- Spine fractures, especially in the neck area. Gently feel and look for any abnormalities. If a spinal injury is sus-

4

pected, stop the secondary survey until the head can be stabilized with sandbags or with rolled blankets or towels.

- Chest fractures and penetrating (sucking) wounds. Observe chest movement. When the sides are not rising together or one side is not moving at all, there may be lung and rib damage.

- Abdominal spasms and tenderness. Gently feel the abdominal area.

- Fractures in the pelvic area. Check for grating, tenderness, bony protrusions, and depressions.

- Fractures or dislocations of the extremities. Check for discoloration, swelling, tenderness, and lumps.

- Paralysis of the extremities. This condition indicates spinal cord damage. Paralysis in the arms and legs indicates a broken neck. Paralysis in the legs, but not arms indicates a broken back. The three checks used to determine this are described in chapter 8.

- Wounds underneath the victim which are often overlooked, especially if the victim is found on his or her back. Check for any bony protrusions or bleeding.

- Burns. Visually examine the victim.

General Principles

Besides being trained in proper first aid methods, all first-aiders should know what first aid equipment is available at the mine site and where it is kept. The equipment should be checked periodically. First aiders should also know the operator's policy for calling medical assistance and transporting the injured.

No two situations requiring first aid are the same, and first-aiders must be able to select and apply appropriate first aid measures in different circumstances. However, the following procedures are generally applicable:

- Take charge: instruct someone to obtain medical help and others to assist as directed.

- Make a primary survey of the victim.

- Care for life-threatening conditions.

- Care for all injuries in order of need.

- If several people have been injured, decide upon priorities in caring for each victim.

- Keep the injured person lying down.

- Loosen restricting clothing when necessary.

- Keep onlookers away from the victim.

- When necessary, improvise first aid materials using the most appropriate material available.

- Cover all wounds completely.

- Use a tourniquet only as necessary.

- Exclude air from burned surfaces as quickly as possible by using a suitable dressing.

- Remove small, loose foreign objects from a wound by brushing away from the wound with a piece of sterile gauze.

- Do not attempt to remove embedded objects.

- Place a bandage compress and a bandage over an open fracture without undue pressure before applying splints.

- Support and immobilize fractures and dislocations.

- Leave the reduction of fractures or dislocations to a doctor except lower jaw dislocations when help is delayed.

- Never move a victim, unless absolutely necessary, until fractures have been immobilized.

- Test a stretcher before use, and carefully place an injured person on the stretcher.

- Carry the victim on a stretcher without any unnecessary rough movements.

Legal Responsibilities

Possible legal implications in rendering first aid care to the sick or injured are sometimes a concern for first-aiders. Since misconceptions surround this area, everyone should have a knowledge of the general principles which govern the actions of first aiders. Because State laws differ widely, first aiders should be familiar with the laws pertaining to emergency care applicable in the State in which they live.

However, there is "Good Samaritan" legislation in almost every State. As long as you are not grossly negligent, do what a reasonable and prudent person would do, and follow the procedures as you are trained in this or another nationally recognized course of instruction, the chances of legal problems are almost nonexistent. To date, no first aider has ever been sued for actions at the site of an accident or sudden illness.

CHAPTER 2. ANATOMY OF THE HUMAN BODY

To understand first aid procedures and to give effective first aid, it is necessary to know something about the anatomy (structure) and physiology (functions) of the human body. The body is composed of solids (bones and tissues) and fluids (blood and the secretions of various glands, organs and membranes).

The principal regions of the body are the head, neck, chest, abdomen, and the upper and lower extremities. For the purposes of first aid training, the upper extremity from the shoulder to the elbow will be referred to as the upper arm or simply the arm. The portion from the elbow to the wrist will be called the forearm. The portion of the lower extremity from the hip to the knee will be called the thigh; and the portion from the knee to the ankle, the leg.

Skeleton

The human skeleton (figure 2.01) is composed of approximately 200 bones, which are classified according to shape as long, short, flat, and irregular bones. The skeleton forms a strong but flexible framework for the body. It supports and carries the soft parts, protects vital organs from injury, gives attachment to muscles and tendons, and forms joints to allow movement.

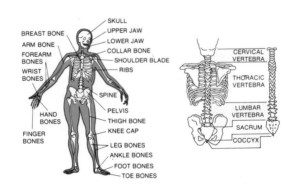

FIGURE 2.01.—The human skeleton.

There are three major divisions of the human skeleton:

—The head.

—The trunk or main part of the body.

—The upper and lower extremities or limbs.

Head

The head is composed of 22 bones, eight of which are closely united to form the skull, a bony case which encloses and protects the brain; 14 other bones form the face. The only movable joint in the head is the lower jaw.

Trunk

The trunk is composed of 54 bones. The spinal column or backbone consists of 24 segments, composed of vertebrae, joined by strong ligaments and cartilage, to form a flexible column that encloses the spinal cord. The chest is formed by 24 ribs, 12 on each side, which are attached in the back to vertebrae. The seven upper pairs of ribs are attached to the breastbone in front by means of cartilage. The next three pairs of ribs are attached in front by a common cartilage to the seventh rib instead of the breastbone. The lower two pairs of ribs, known as the floating ribs, are not attached in front.

The pelvis is a basin-shaped bony structure at the lower portion of the trunk. The pelvis is below the movable vertebrae of the spinal column, which it supports, and above the lower limbs, upon which it rests. Four bones compose the pelvis, the two bones of the backbone and the wing-shaped hip bones on either side. The pelvis forms the floor of the abdominal cavity and provides deep sockets in which the heads of the thigh bones fit.

Extremities

Each upper extremity consists of 32 bones. The collarbone is a long bone, the inner end of which is fastened to the breastbone and the outer end is fastened to the shoulder blade at the shoulder joint. The collarbone lies just in front of and above the first rib. The shoulder blade is a flat triangular bone which lies at the upper and outer part of the back of the chest and forms part of the shoulder joint. The arm bone extends from the shoulder to the elbow. The two bones of the forearm extend from the elbow to the wrist. There are eight wrist bones, five bones in the palm of the hand, and 14 finger bones, two in the thumb and three in each finger.

Each lower extremity consists of 30 bones. The thigh bone, the longest and strongest bone in the body, extends from the hip joint to the knee; its upper end is rounded to fit into the socket in the pelvis, and its lower end broadens out to help form part of the knee joint. The kneecap is buried in the large tendon which crosses the front of the knee joint. This flat triangular bone can be felt moving in front of the knee joint. The two bones in the leg extend from the knee joint to the ankle. There are seven bones of the ankle and back part of the foot, five long bones of the front part of the foot, and 14 toe bones.

Most fractures and dislocations occur to the bones and joints in the extremities.

Joints and Ligaments

Two or more bones coming together form a joint. There are three types of joints:

1. Immovable joints, such as those in the skull.

2. Joints with limited motion, such as those of the ribs and lower spine.

3. Freely movable joints, such as the knee, ankle, elbow, etc.

Freely movable joints, which are most commonly injured, are of most concern in first aid. The ends of bones forming a movable joint are covered by cartilage, and the bones are held in place by strong white bands, called ligaments, extending from one bone to another and entirely around the joint (figure 2.02). A smooth membrane that lines the end of the cartilage and the inside of the ligaments secretes a fluid that keeps the joints lubricated.

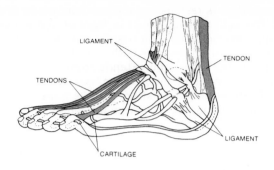

FIGURE 2.02.—Ligaments and tendons of the foot.

Muscles and Tendons

Bones, the framework of the body, are mostly covered with flesh and muscle tissue which give the body its shape and contour.

There are two types of muscle:

1. Voluntary muscles are those that are consciously controlled, such as muscles of the arms and legs.

2. Involuntary muscles are those that are not consciously controlled, such as muscles of the heart and those that control digestion and breathing.

Strong, inelastic, fibrous cords called tendons attach the muscles to the bones. The muscles cause the bones to move by flexing or extending.

Skin

The skin is the body's protective covering; it also contains the sweat glands which help regulate body temperature. The skin consists of three layers, an external layer (epidermis), a deep layer or true skin (dermis), and the fat tissue layer (subcutaneous). The skin is one of the most important organs of the body. The loss of a large part of the skin will result in death unless it can be replaced.

The protective functions of the skin are numerous. Skin is watertight and keeps internal fluids in while keeping germs out. Information is carried to the brain through a system of nerves in the skin. These nerves transmit information about pain, external pressure, heat, cold, and the relative position of various parts of the body (figure 2.03).

Skin provides information to the first-aider concerning victim's condition. For example, pale, sweaty skin may indicate shock.

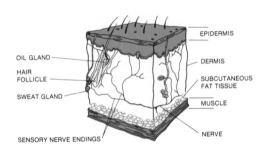

OIL GLAND

HAIR FOLLICLE

SWEAT GLAND

SENSORY NERVE ENDINGS

EPIDERMIS

DERMIS

SUBCUTANEOUS FAT TISSUE

MUSCLE

NERVE

FIGURE 2.03.—Skin.

Chest Cavity

The chest cavity (figure 2.04) is cone-shaped. It is formed by the upper part of the spinal column or backbone at the back, the ribs on the sides, and the ribs and breastbone in front. A thin, muscular partition at the bottom, the diaphragm, separates the chest cavity and the abdominal cavity. The diaphragm is dome-shaped and lower in the back than in the front.

The lungs and the heart occupy most of the chest cavity. The heart lies between the lungs, in the center of the chest behind the breastbone. It is positioned slightly to the left side, making the left lung smaller than the right. Besides the heart and the lungs, the chest cavity contains the food pipe (esophagus), the windpipe (trachea), and several major blood vessels.

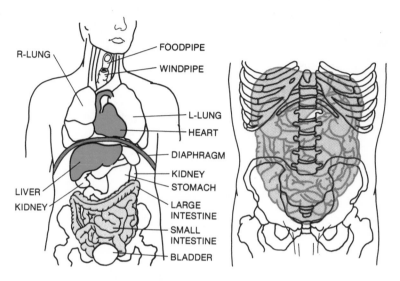

Figure 2.04.—Chest and abdominal cavities.

Abdominal Cavity

The abdominal cavity (figure 2.04) is in the lower portion of the trunk. It is formed by the lower portion of the backbone, the muscles in the back, and abdominal muscles at the sides and front. The diaphragm forms the top of the cavity and the pelvic basin forms the bottom.

The abdomen contains many important organs: the liver in the upper right portion; the stomach and the spleen in the upper left portion; the small and large intestines in the lower portion; the kidneys, one on each side, in the back; and the urinary bladder in the pelvic region.

There are also major blood vessels and other organs in the abdominal cavity.

Excretory Systems

The waste products that enter the body or are formed within it are eliminated by several different systems. The residue of food taken into the digestive system, mainly indigestible materials, together with secretions from various glands emptying into the intestines, is gathered in the lower portion of the large intestine and eliminated through the rectum as feces.

Excess water carrying dissolved salts which are either in excess in the system or formed as waste products is extracted by the kidneys, collected in the bladder, and expelled as urine.

Carbon dioxide and certain volatile products carried by the blood are exchanged in the lungs for oxygen and pass from the body in exhaled air.

The skin contains many small organs known as sweat glands. They range from 400 to 2,800 per square inch, over different parts of the body. These glands are important in eliminating heat, excess fluid, and dissolved waste products from the body.

Life and health depend on the body giving off its waste products; interference with the normal functioning of any of the excretory systems results in illness and may even cause death.

CHAPTER 3. ARTIFICIAL VENTILATION

Respiratory System

Oxygen is essential to human life; all living tissue depends on the oxygen carried by the blood. Oxygen enters the body through respiration, the breathing process. Any interference with breathing produces oxygen depletion (anoxia) throughout the entire body. Knowledge of the respiratory system and the organs concerned with respiration will greatly aid in understanding artificial ventilation.

During respiration, when air is taken into the lungs (inhalation) and forced out (exhalation), the air passes through the nose, throat, and windpipe. The air is warmed and moistened in the nose. The moist hairs and moist mucous membrane of the nose filter out much of the dust in inhaled air.

The throat is a continuation of the nose and mouth. At its lower end are two openings, one in front of the other. The opening in front is called the trachea or windpipe and leads to the lungs. The one behind is called the esophagus or food pipe and leads to the stomach (figure 3.01).

At the top of the windpipe is a flap, the epiglottis, which closes over the windpipe during swallowing to keep food or liquid from entering it. When a person is unconscious, the flap fails to respond; therefore, no solids or liquids should be given by mouth, since they may enter the windpipe or the lungs and cause strangulation or serious complications. The tongue of an unconscious person, especially if the person is lying on his or her back, is apt to fall against the back of the throat and interfere with air reaching the lungs. In some cases, it may block the throat entirely. When a person is unconscious or breathing with difficulty, the chin should always be extended. This brings the tongue forward.

The windpipe extends into the chest cavity where it divides into the two bronchial tubes, one going to each lung. Within the lungs, the tubes branch out like limbs of a tree, until they become very small.

15

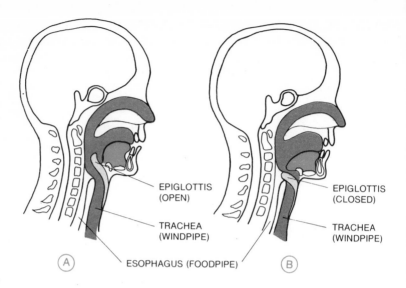

FIGURE 3.01.—Nose, throat, trachea, and esophagus.
A, Epiglottis closed; B, epiglottis open.

The lungs are two cone-shaped bodies that are soft, spongy, and elastic. Each lung is covered by a closed sac called the pleura. The inside of the lungs communicates freely with the outside air through the windpipe.

During breathing the chest muscles and diaphragm expand the chest cavity, so that the air pressure within the chest cavity becomes less than that outside. Air rushes to balance the pressure, filling the lungs.

If any air gets through the chest wall, or if the lung is punctured so that air from the outside can fill the pleural space, the lungs will not fill. This is because the air pressure is equal outside and inside the chest cavity. Thus no suction is created on inhaling.

After subdividing into very small branches, the bronchial tubes and in a group of air cells (alveoli) resembling a very small bunch of grapes. Around each of the air cells, which have very thin walls, is a fine network of small blood vessels or capillaries. The blood in these capillaries releases carbon dioxide and other waste matter, the by-products of tissue activity from all over the body, through the thin air-cell wall and, in exchange takes on a supply of oxygen from the air breathed into the air cells. The discarded carbon dioxide and waste matter leave the air cells in the exhaled air (figure 3.02).

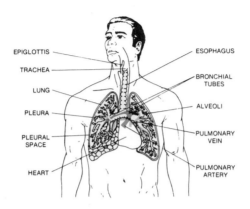

FIGURE 3.02.—Respiratory system.

Breathing is an act which usually is automatic and one over which a person exerts only a certain degree of control. The amount of air breathed and frequency of breathing vary according to whether the person is at rest or engaged in work or exercise. At rest, a healthy adult breathes between 12 and 15 times a minute and takes in 25 to 30 cubic inches of air per breath. During strenuous work, the breathing rate and amount inhaled may be increased several times.

Breathing consists of two separate acts; inhalation, enlarging the chest cavity so air is drawn into the lungs, and exhalation, decreasing the size of the chest cavity so air is driven out of the lungs.

During inhalation the ribs are raised and the arch of the diaphragm falls and becomes flattened, increasing the capacity of the chest cavity, and causing air to enter (A of figure 3.03). In inhalation, an act performed with slignt muscular action, the ribs fall to their normal position, the arch of the diaphragm rises decreasing the capacity of the chest cavity, and air is forced out (B of figure 3.03).

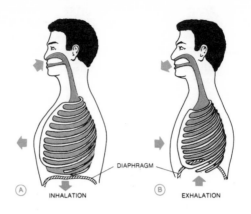

FIGURE 3.03.—Breathing process.
A, inhalation phase; B, exhalation phase.

Causes of Respiratory Arrest

Breathing may stop as a result of a variety of serious accidents. The most common causes of respiratory arrest are electric shock, drowning, suffocation, poisonous gases, head injuries, and heart problem.

FIGURE 3.04.—Causes of respiratory arrest.

Electric Shock

The chance of accidental contact with electrical current is a common hazard in and around mines. Any electric current may be dangerous. Electricity can cause paralysis of the nerve centers that control breathing and stop or alter the regular beat of the heart.

The symptoms of electric shock are sudden loss of consciousness, impairment or absence of respiration and/or circulation, weak pulse, and sometimes burns. If breathing is present, it is frequently so weak and shallow that it cannot be detected.

If the victim is free from contact with the electric current, begin first aid care at once. If the victim is still in contact with the current, rescue the victim at once, being careful not to come in contact with the current. Every second of delay in removing a person from contact with an electric current lessens the chance of resuscitation. It is essential to act quickly but always in a way that protects the rescuer from contact. The current should be turned off if possible, but no time should be spent looking for a switch. A dry board, thick dry paper, or cloth should be used to stand on. A dry belt, hankerchief, or a piece of rope can be looped over the foot or other part of the body to pull the victim from the current. Or a nonconductive material can be used to remove the current source from the victim. In all cases, the current should be removed from the victim or the victim from the current promptly (figure 3.05). Artificial ventilation or CPR should be started at once, if necessary.

FIGURE 3.05.—Removing victim from contact with electric current.

The following precautions help prevent accidental contact with electric current:

- Replace worn out or damaged power tools, appliances, motors, fixture outlets, and cords.

- Inspect electric cables periodically for defects.

- Be sure that equipment is properly grounded.

- Don't work on energized circuits.

- Avoid working alone when using electrical equipment.

- Keep yourself and your equipment dry.

- Don't overload or abuse electrical equipment or circuits.

If there is any question as to the condition of electric circuits or equipment, do not use them until a qualified person has checked and made the necessary repairs.

Drowning

A victim of drowning should be removed from the water as quickly as possible. Artificial ventilation should begin immediately without taking the time to remove water which may be in the respiratory tract.

Drowning is a form of suffocation. The supply of air to the lungs has been cut off completely by water or spasm of the larnyx. This cutoff does not create an immediate lack of oxygen in the body. There is a small reserve in the air cells of the lungs, in the blood, and in some of the tissue that can sustain life for up to six minutes or longer at low temperatures. Because this reserve is exhausted relatively quickly, it is important to start artificial ventilation as soon as possible. Care should be taken that the nose and mouth are lower than the chest.

- Always wear a lifejacket or other flotation device when working around water.

- Don't overestimate your ability to swim; judging distance accurately over water is very difficult.

- Never swim alone.

- Don't swim in unfamiliar areas, which may harbor unknown dangerous currents, deep holes, debris, or other hazards.

- Do not swim when overtired, overheated, or immediately after eating.

- Before diving into the water, make sure it is deep enough and there are no objects hidden beneath the surface.

Suffocation

Always rescue a suffocation victim as quickly as possible. Symptoms of suffocation in an unconscious person are that lips, fingernail ends, and ear lobes become blue or darker in color, the pulse becomes rapid and weak, breathing stops, and the pupils of the eyes become dilated. The cause is a blocked windpipe preventing air from getting into the lungs, artificial ventilation is of no value until blockage is removed.

The following precautions help prevent suffocation:

- Follow all safe operating procedures when entering bins and hoppers. working on or near stockpiles, and in trenching operations.

- Cut food into small pieces, eat slowly, chew thoroughly, and watch out for small pieces of bone, seed, or shell. The most common cause of suffocation in adults in swallowing large pieces of food while under the influence of alcohol.

- Never wear defective dentures.

- Do not sleep with gum or tobacco in your mouth.

- Children should never be allowed to put foreign objects in their mouths. Keep all pieces of plastic away from children.

- Provide children with sturdy, safe toys that don't have small parts that might become detached.

- Remove bones and shells from all food given to children.

- Never give children under the age of 4, nuts, uncooked vegetables, fruits that require chewing, unchopped meat or foods that have pits or seeds.

- Never run, laugh, or talk with food in your mouth.

Dangerous Gases

Several noxious or toxic gases encountered in the mining, metallurgical, petroleum, and allied industries, as well as in everyday life, can cause suffocation. These gases include carbon monoxide, sulfur dioxide, oxides of nitrogen, ammonia, hydrogen cyanide, and cyanogen compounds. Persons should be aware of the *early* warning signs of exposure, so gases may be deterred before suffocation occurs. Headache and nausea are the two most common symptoms of the presence of dangerous gases. Rescuers should take care to protect themselves. Unless the surrounding air is good, the victim should be taken to pure air immediately and aritifical ventilation began at once.

The following precautions should be taken to prevent poisoning by toxic or noxious gases in mines and plants:

- Maintain ventilation to dilute and carry away the gases.

- Avoid exposure to air known to contain poisonous gases.

- Use adequate protective equipment when atmospheres known to contain poisonous gases are to be entered.

- Use proper testing devices before entering an area where dangerous gases could exist.

Principles of Artifical Ventilation

Artifical ventilation is the process for causing air flow into and from the lungs when natural breathing has ceased or when it is very irregular or inadequate.

When breathing has ceased, so that the body's oxygen supply is cut off the brain cells may start to die within four to six minutes. This process may result in irreversible brain damage and if breathing is not restored, in death. In some cases the heart may continue to beat and circulate blood for a short period after a person stops breathing. In these cases life can transport the oxygen to the body's tissues. If artificial ventilation is started within a short time after respiratory arrest, the victim has a good change for survival (figure 3.06).

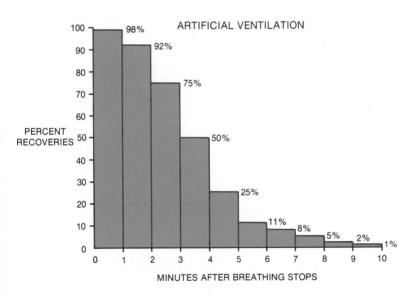

FIGURE 3.06.—Recovery rate.

Certain general principles must always be kept in mind when administering artificial ventilation by any method:

- Time is of prime importance; every second counts.

- Do not take time to move the victim unless the site of the respiratory arrest is hazardous.

- Do not delay ventilation to loosen the victim's clothing or warm the victim; these are secondary in importance to getting air into the victim's lungs.

- If possible, place the victim's head at a slight downhill angle to permit better drainage of fluids.

- Sweep back of throat with index or middle finger to remove all foreign objects, such as food, gum, loose dentures, tobacco or any other loose material.

- See that the chin is extended, which will bring the tongue forward.

- An assistant should loosen any tight fitting clothing in order to promote circulation and go or send for help.

- Keep the victim warm by covering with a blanket, clothing, or other material.

- Maintain a steady, constant rhythm while providing artificial ventilation. Be sure to look for rise and fall of the chest and look, listen, and feel for return air; if none, look for upper airway obstruction.

- The cycle of ventilation should never be interrupted.

- Continue artifical ventilation until one of the following occurs:
    1. Spontaneous breathing resumes.
    2. You are relieved by a qualified person.
    3. A doctor pronounces the victim dead.
    4. When the rescuer is exhausted and unable to continue.

- Do not fight the victim's attempts to breathe.

- Once the victim recovers, constantly monitor the victim's condition because breathing may stop again.

- The victim should be kept in a semi-reclining position.

- Treat the victim for physical shock.

Obstructed Airway

An obstruction in the airway can result in unconsciousness and respiratory arrest. Approximately 3000 people die annually from obstruction of the airway by a foreign body. Any large foreign object such as gum, tobacco, or loose dentures can block the airway, but foreign body obstruction generally occurs during eating. Meat is the most common cause, but a variety of other foods can cause choking. The most common factors associated with choking while eating are the following:

—The influence of alcohol.

—Dentures.

—Large, poorly chewed pieces of food.

The most common cause of airway obstruction in an unconscious person is the tongue falling back into the airway.

Maneuvers to Remove an Obstruction

If conscious, allow the victim to attempt to remove the obstruction.

The following, in order of priority, are techniques that the rescuer may use to remove an obstruction from the airway,

- Manual removal.

- Blows to the back.

- Manual thrusts to the abdomen and chest.

- Combination of back blows and manual thrusts.

Manual Removal

Whenever a foreign object is in the victim's mouth, it should be removed by the rescuer using the fingers. Back blows and manual thrusts may dislodge the obstruction, but not expel it. The rescuer should turn the victim's head away, open the victim's mouth with the cross finger technique if necessary (figure 3.15), and clear the obstruction with a finger sweep.

Cross-Finger Technique

- Cross your thumb under your index finger.

- Brace your thumb and finger against the victim's upper and lower teeth.

- Push your fingers apart to separate the jaws. (figure 3.07).

FIGURE 3.07.—Cross-finger technique.

Finger Sweep

- Open the victim's jaws with the cross-finger technique, if necessary.

- Insert the index finger of your other hand down the inside of the cheek and into the throat to the base of the tongue.

- The index finger is then swept across the back of the throat in a hooking action to dislodge the obstruction.

- Grasp and remove the foreign object when it comes within reach (figure 3.08).

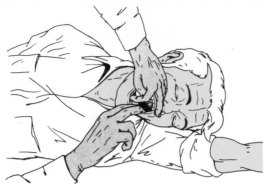
FIGURE 3.08.—Finger sweep.

Blows to the Back

Sharp blows delivered between the shoulder blades in rapid succession with the heel of the hand may relieve a blockage of the airway. Blows to the back can be administered with the victim in a sitting, standing, or lying position. When administering back blows the victim's head should be at chest level or lower.

Victim Sitting or Standing

- Position yourself at the side and slightly behind the victim.

- Place one hand on the front of the victim's chest for support.

- Lean victim forward so that the head is chest level or lower.

- Deliver several sharp blows with the heel of the hand to the victim's spine between the shoulder blades (figure 3.09).

FIGURE 3.09.—Blows to the back with the victim sitting.

Victim Lying

- Kneel and roll the victim so that the victim's chest rests against your knees.

- Deliver several sharp blows with the heel of the hand to the victim's spine between the shoulder blades (figure 3.10).

FIGURE 3.10.—Blows to the back with victim lying.

Manual Thrusts

A rapid series of manual thrusts to the upper abdomen (abdominal thrust) or lower chest (chest thrust) may relieve a foreign body obstruction. The chest thrust should be used for an obese person or a pregnant woman.

Abdominal Thrust

Victim Sitting or Standing

- Stand behind the victim and place your arms around the victim's waist.

- Grasp one fist in your other hand and position the thumb side of your fist against the middle of the victim's abdomen between the rib cage and the navel.

- Press your fist into the victim's abdominal area with a quick upward thrust (figure 3.11).

- Repeat the procedure if necessary.

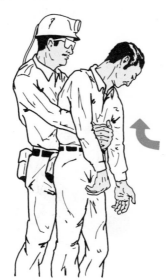

FIGURE 3.11.—Abdominal thrust with victim standing.

Victim Lying Down

- Position the victim on his or her back.

- Kneel close to the victim's hips.

- Place the heel of one hand against the middle of the victim's abdomen between the rib cage and the navel with fingers pointing toward the victim's chest.

- Place your other hand on top of the first.

- Move your shoulders directly over the victim's abdomen.

- Press into the victim's abdominal area with a quick upward thrust (figure 3.12).

- Repeat the procedure if necessary.

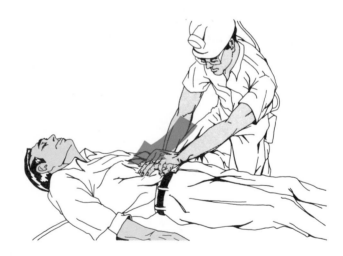

FIGURE 3.12.—Abdominal thrust with victim lying.

Victim Alone

The victim of an obstructed airway, who is alone, may use his or her own fist, as described above, or bend over the back of a chair and exert downward pressure.

FIGURE 3.13.—Abdominal thrust using a chair.

Chest Thrust

The chest thrust is another method of applying the manual thrust for removing an obstruction from the airway. This method is used when the rescuer is unable to wrap his or her arms around the victim's waist, as in advanced pregnancy or gross obesity.

Victim Sitting or Standing

- Stand behind the victim and wrap your arms around the victim's lower chest.

- Grasp one fist with your other hand and position the thumb side of your fist on the lower sternum, about armpit level.

- Press into the victim's chest with a quick backward thrust. (figure 3.14).

- Repeat the procedure if necessary.

FIGURE 3.14.—Chest thrust with victim standing.

Victim Lying

- Position the victim on his/her back.

- Open the airway and turn the head to the side.

- Kneel close to the victim.

- Place the heel of one hand on the lower half of the breast bone about 1 to 1½ inches above the tip with fingers elevated. The long axis of the heel of the hand must be parallel to the breast bone.

- Place the other hand on top of and parallel to the first hand.

- With your shoulders over your hands, exert a downward thrust with arm and shoulder movement (figure 3.15).

- Repeat the procedure if necessary.

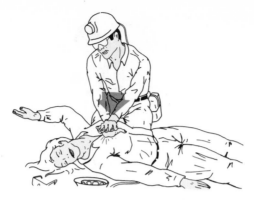

FIGURE 3.15.—Chest thrust with victim lying down.

Combination of Back Blows and Manual Thrusts

Blows to the victim's back instantaneously increase pressure in the airway, which may either partially or completely dislodge an obstruction. Manual thrusts produce a lower but more sustained increase in pressure in the airway and may further aid in dislodging an obstruction. Using back blows followed by manual thrusts is generally the most efficient method of clearing an obstruction from the airway.

Infants and Small Children

- Place the child face down over your forearm with the child's head lower than the rest of the body.

- Deliver several moderate blows with the heel of the hand to the spine between the shoulder blades (figure 3.16).

33

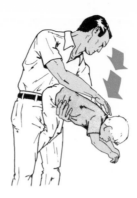

FIGURE 3.16.—Blows to the back of an infant or small child.

Methods of Artificial Ventilation

The first thing to do when coming upon an unconscious person is to establish unresponsiveness by tapping on the shoulder and asking "Are you OK?" The victim should then be placed on his or her back. All foreign objects, such as loose dentures, tobacco, gum, and any loose material should be quickly removed from the victim's mouth (A of figure 3.17). Then check for breathing by tilting the head and looking at the chest for movement, listing for air movement, and feeling chest movement. Afterwards, if no air movement is detected, lift under the neck and tilt the crown of the head downwards. Another way to open the airway is to tilt the head and pull the lower jaw so that the chin points straight up. This pulls the tongue forward so that the air passage is open. Sometimes the victim will then resume breathing (B of figure 3.17). If the victim is still not breathing, start resuscitation at once. Any delay may prove fatal.

Traditionally, four methods of artificial ventilation have been taught for use on a victim of respiratory arrest: mouth-to-mouth, Holger-Nielsen (back pressure, arm lift), Schafer (prone pressure), and Silvester. Mouth-to-mouth ventilation is by far the most effective means of artificial ventilation. Although the other manual methods work, they are not nearly as efficient. They do not provide as much air and it is more difficult to maintain an open airway. Unless there are special circumstances, such as severe facial injuries, that require the use of another method, mouth-to-mouth ventilation should be used.

Mouth-to-Mouth Ventilation

The most important principle in mouth-to-mouth ventilation is to keep the victim's head and neck properly extended to allow adequate passage in the throat for air to enter the lungs.

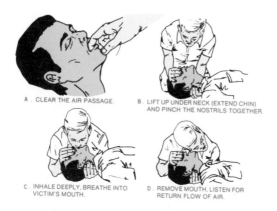

A . CLEAR THE AIR PASSAGE.

B . LIFT UP UNDER NECK (EXTEND CHIN) AND PINCH THE NOSTRILS TOGETHER.

C . INHALE DEEPLY, BREATHE INTO VICTIM'S MOUTH.

D . REMOVE MOUTH, LISTEN FOR RETURN FLOW OF AIR.

FIGURE 3.17.—Mouth-to-mouth ventilation.

- Pinch the nostrils together to prevent loss of air through the nose (B of figure 3.17).

- Inhale deeply (C of figure 3.17).

- Place your mouth over the victim's mouth (over mouth and nose with children) making sure of a tight seal. Blow into the air passage until the victim's chest rises.

- Keep the victim's head extended at all times.

- Remove your mouth and let the victim exhale (D of figure 3.17).

- Feel and listen for the return flow of air, and look for a fall of the victim's chest.

Repeat this operation 12 times a minute for an adult and 20 times a minute for a small child.

Mouth-to-Nose Ventilation

In certain cases, mouth-to-nose ventilation may be required. The mouth-to-nose technique is similar to mouth-to-mouth except that the lips are sealed by pushing the lower jaw against the upper jaw and air is then forced into the victim by way of the nose (figure. 3.18).

FIGURE 3.18.—Mouth-to-nose ventilation.

Mouth-to-Stoma Ventilation

Mouth-to-stoma ventilation must be used for a victim who has had a laryngectomy (figure 3.19). A laryngectomy is the removal of the larynx (voice box or "Adams Apple") by surgery.

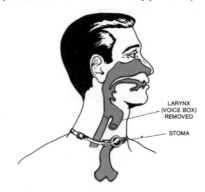

FIGURE 3.19.—Laryngectomy.

The same procedures as for mouth-to-mouth ventilation are used for mouth-to-stoma ventilation, except that the rescuer's mouth is placed directly over the stoma (figure 3.20). The head tilt and pinching the nose closed are not necessary. This victim no longer breathes through the mouth or nose.

FIGURE 3.20.—Mouth-to-stoma ventilation.

Holger-Nielsen (Back Pressure, Arm Lift) Method

The Holger-Nielsen (back pressure, arm lift) method relies on manual pressures to imitate the natural breathing process.

Steps in the Holger-Nielsen Method

- Place the victim face down, with the victim's elbows bent and the victim's hands placed one upon the other, under the head.

- Turn the victim's head slightly to one side, so the cheek rests on the victim's hand.

- Kneel on one or both knees at the victim's head.

- Place your hands on the victim's back just below an imaginary line between the armpits; the tips of the thumbs should be just touching and the fingers spread downward and outward (figure 3.21).

37

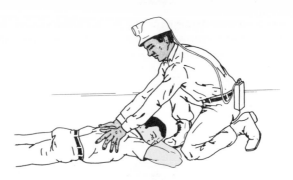

FIGURE 3.21.—Holger-Neilsen method: correct position of victim and operator.

- Rock forward and press on the victim's back until your arms are approximately vertical.

- Allow the weight of the upper body to exert slow, steady, even pressure upon the hands. Keep the elbows straight, and exert pressure almost directly downward on the victim's back (figure 3.22).

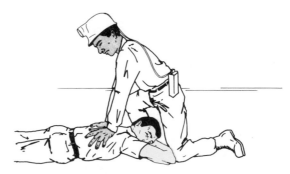

FIGURE 3.22.—Holger-Neilsen method: downward pressure.

- Release the pressure, avoiding a final thrust.

- Grasp the victim's elbows and pull them toward you by rocking backward slowly. Apply enough lift to feel resistance and tension in the victim's shoulders. Keep your own elbows straight while rocking backward, and draw the victim's elbows up and towards you as a natural part of sitting back (figure 3.23).

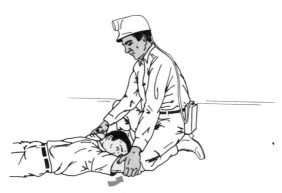

FIGURE 3.23.—Holger-Neilsen method: inhalation phase.

- Lower the victim's elbows to the ground.

- Replace your arms at the starting position and repeat the cycle at a rate of 12 times per minute.

Changing Operators in the Holger-Nielsen Method

In performing artificial ventilation for long periods, the operator becomes tired, making relief necessary.

There are a number of ways to change operators. It should always be done without altering the rhythm of the stroke. If possible, about the same pressure should be maintained on the victim by each operator.

One suggested method is as follows:

- The relief operator kneels on one knee beside the operator and the victim, facing the operator (A of figure 3.24).

- The relief operator swings sideways in unison with the operator, picking up the rhythm of the stroke. This should be done for three or four strokes (B of figute 3.24).

- At a prearranged signal at the end of a cycle as the victim's arms are lowered to the ground, the operator swings to one side, out of the way.

- The relief operator, resting on one knee, swings into place with hands in the proper position on the victim's back (C of figure 3.24).

- The relief operator is now ready to continue the operation.

FIGURE 3.24.—Shafer method.

SHAFER (Prone Pressure) Method

The Shafer (prone pressure) method, like the Holger-Neilsen method, relies on manual pressure to force air out of the lungs. Air enters the lungs when pressure is released and the chest expands.

Steps in the Shafer Method

- Lay the victim face down, with one arm extended directly over the head and the other arm bent at the elbow.

- Turn the victim's head toward the extended arm so that the side of the head is lying on the hand or forearm of the bent arm.

- Kneel, straddling the victim's hips, thigh, or thighs, in a position that will allow you to place the palms of your hands on the small of the victim's back (figure 3.25).

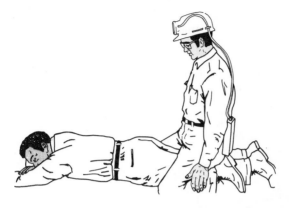

FIGURE 3.25.—Shafer method: correct positioning of victim and operator.

- The fingers should rest on the ribs, the little finger just touching the lowest, floating rib, the thumb and fingers in a natural position, with the tips of the fingers just out of sight on the sides of the trunk (figure 3.26).

FIGURE 3.26.—Shafer method: hand positioning for compressions.

- With your arms held straight, swing forward slowly, so that the weight of your body is gradually brought to bear upon the victim.

- Your shoulders should be directly over the heels of the hands at the end of the forward swing.

- Do not bend the elbows.

FIGURE 3.27.—Shafer method: compression phase.

- Swing backward immediately to remove the pressure completely.

- After two seconds, replace the hands and swing forward again.

- Repeat this procedure 12 times a minute.

Changing Operators in the Shafer Method

The sequence of steps in order to change operators in the Shafer method is as follows:

- The relief operator kneels beside the victim and swings forward and backward in unison with the operator.

- At a prearranged backward motion or decompression phase, the operator swings off the victim to the side opposite the relief operator.

- At the same time, the relief operator swings into position straddling the victim's thigh or thighs to make the next compression stroke.

Silvester Method

The Silvester method of artificial ventilation makes use of the muscles used in regular respiration to force air into and out of the lungs.

Steps in the Silvester Method

- Place the victim on his or her back.

- Remove all foreign objects, such as loose dentures, tobacco, gum, and food from the victim's mouth.

- Place a rolled-up coat or pad under the victim's shoulders. This will tilt the head back, move the tongue away from the back of the throat, and straighten the windpipe.

- Turn the victim's head to the side.

- Kneel at the victim's head.

- Grasp both the victim's arms at the back of the wrists (A of figure 3.28).

- Bring the arms forward over the chest, and bend at the elbows, and bring forearms parallel to each other.

- Keeping your arms straight, continue until your shoulders are directly under your hands and rock forward with moderately increasing pressure. Press down to decrease the size of the chest (B of figure 3.28).

- Draw the victim's arms upward and outward gently and hold them as far as they will go above the victim's head. This motion opens and expands the chest to the greatest possible extent.

- Repeat this cycle at a rate of 12 times per minute.

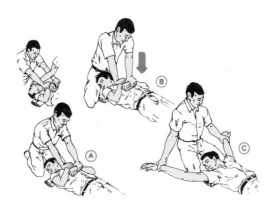

FIGURE 3.28.—Silvester method.

Changing Operators in the Silvester Method

When done properly, this method is hard work for the operator, who should be relieved as soon as tired. Changing operators should be done in a way that avoids any change in rhythm.

- The relief operator kneels beside the operator and grasps the nearest wrist, just below and partially overlapping the operator's hand.

- The relief operator matches the operator's motion for three or four cycles to gain the rhythm of the stroke.

- At a prearranged signal, and at the end of the compression stroke, the operator lets go and swings to one side.

- The relief operator, resting on one knee, swings into place, properly holding the victim's wrist.

Administration of Oxygen

When the victim begins to breathe normally, supplemental oxygen can be administered. Oxygen may be available in compressed form in an oxygen bottle or cylinder. The bottle or cylinder valve should be opened slightly, with the oxygen flow directed away from the victim. After a moderate flow has been established, the oxygen should be directed past the victim's nose. A cap, hat, or piece of cloth may be used as an improvised mask to confine the oxygen to the victim's face. An oxygen inhaler aids in administration. Smoking and open flame must not be allowed in the area when oxygen is being administered. Since there are a number of kinds of supplemental oxygen units, the rescuer should become familiar with the unit available at the work place.

CHAPTER 4. CONTROL OF BLEEDING

Circulatory System

The circulatory system (figure 4.01), by which blood is carried to and from all parts of the body, consists of the heart and blood vessels. Through the blood vessels, blood is circulated to and from all parts of the body under pressure supplied by the pumping action of the heart.

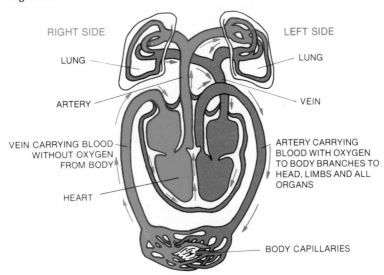

FIGURE 4.01.—Circulatory system.

Blood

Blood is composed of serum or plasma, red cells, white cells, and platelets. Plasma is a fluid which carries the blood cells and transports nutrients to all tissues. It also transports waste products resulting from tissue activity to the organs of excretion. Red cells give color to the blood and carry oxygen. White cells aid in defending the body against infection. Platelets are essential to the formation of blood clots, which are necessary to stop bleeding.

One-twelfth to one-fifteenth of the body weight is blood. A person weighing 150 pounds will have approximately 10 to 12 pints of blood. If the blood supply is cut off from tissues, they will die from lack of oxygen. The loss of two pints, 8 to 10 percent of the body's blood, by an adult usually is serious, and the loss of three pints may be fatal if it occurs over a short time, one to two hours. At certain points in the body, fatal hemorrhages may occur in a very short time. The cutting of the two principal blood vessels in the neck, the principal blood vessels in the arm, or the principal blood vessels in the thigh may cause hemorrhage that will prove fatal in one to three minutes or even less. Rupture of the main trunk blood vessels of the chest and abdomen may cause fatal hemorrhage in less than thirty seconds.

The loss of blood causes a state of physical shock. This occurs because there is insufficient blood flowing through the tissues of the body to provide food and oxygen. All processes of the body are affected. When a person is in shock, vital body functions slow down. If the conditions causing shock are not reversed, death may result.

Blood Vessels

Oxygenated blood is carried from the heart by a large artery (figure 4.02) called the aorta. Smaller arteries branch off from this large artery, and those arteries in turn branch off into still smaller arteries. These arteries divide and subdivide until they become very small, ending in threadlike vessels known as capillaries, which extend into all the organs and tissues.

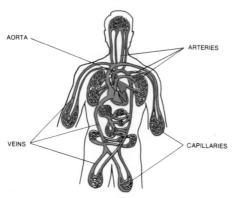

FIGURE 4.02.—The blood vessels.

47

After the blood has furnished the necessary nourishment and oxygen to the tissues and organs of the body, it takes on waste products, particularly carbon dioxide. The blood returns to the heart by means of a different system of blood vessels known as veins. The veins are connected with the arteries through the capillaries.

Very small veins join, forming larger veins, which in turn join until the very largest veins return the blood to the heart. While the blood is returning to the heart, it passes through the kidneys, where waste products are removed. When the blood from the body reaches the heart, carbon dioxide and other volatile waste products contained in the blood but not removed by the kidneys must be eliminated and the oxygen used by the body replaced. The heart pumps the blood delivered to it by the veins into the lungs, where it flows through another network of capillaries. There, the carbon dioxide and other waste products are exchanged for oxygen through the delicate walls of air cells. Thus, the blood is oxygenated and ready to return to the heart, which recirculates it throughout the body (figure 4.01). The time taken for the blood to make one complete circulation of the body through miles and miles of blood vessels, is approximately 75 seconds in an adult at rest.

Heart

The heart is a hollow, muscular organ about the size of a fist, and lies in the lower central region of the chest cavity. By the heart's pumping action, blood is kept under pressure and in constant circulation throughout the body. In a healthy adult at rest, the heart contracts between 60 and 80 times a minute; in a child, 80 to 100 times per minute. The effect of these contractions can be noted by means of the pulse, a spurt of blood through an artery as shown in (figure 4.03). The pulse is most easily felt over the carotid artery on either side of the neck. The usual place to take the pulse is on the thumb side of the inner surface of the wrist, but it is often difficult to find in an emergency, as the artery is small and quite a distance from the heart (figure 4.04).

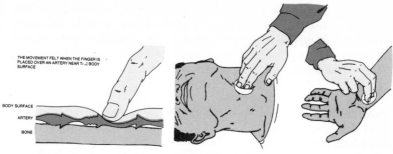

FIGURE 4.03.—Pulse.　　FIGURE 4.04—Checking the pulse.

The heart may be likened to a four-cylinder pump, except that the "cylinders" of the heart do not discharge into a common outlet. Figure 4.05 illustrates schematically the flow of the blood through the heart. "Cylinder" 1 draws the deoxygenated or venous blood from all parts of the body and passes it into "cylinder" 2. "Cylinder" 2 pumps the impure blood to the blood vessels of the lungs. "Cylinder" 3 draws the blood from the lungs back to the heart and passes it into "cylinder" 4. Through the strong action of "cylinder" 4 the blood starts out on a new trip through the arteries.

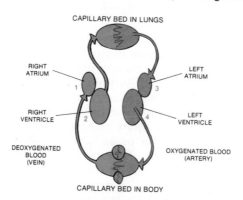

FIGURE 4.05.—Oxygenation of the blood.

Hemorrhage or Bleeding

Hemorrhage or bleeding is a flow of blood from an artery, vein, or capillary. In severe bleeding, place the patient in such a position that he or she will be least affected by the loss of blood. Lay the victim down and elevate the victim's legs in a semi-flexed position. This prevents aggravation of spinal injury or breathing impairment (figure 4.06). Control the bleeding. Maintain an open airway and give the victim plenty of fresh air. Prevent the loss of body heat by putting blankets under and over the victim. The victim should be kept at rest, as movement will increase heart action, which causing the blood to flow faster, and perhaps interfering with clot formation or dislodging a clot already formed.

FIGURE 4.06.—Position of victim for severe bleeding.

Bleeding from an Artery

When bright red blood spurts from a wound, an artery has been cut. The blood in the arteries comes directly from the heart, and spurts at each contraction. Having received a fresh supply of oxygen, the blood is bright red (figure 4.07).

Bleeding from a Vein

When dark red blood flows from a wound in steady stream, a vein has been cut. The blood, having given up its oxygen and received carbon dioxide and waste products in return, is dark red (figure 4.07).

Bleeding from Capillaries

When blood oozes from a wound, capillaries have been cut. There is usually no cause for alarm, relatively little blood can be lost. Usually direct pressure with a compress applied over the wound will cause the formation of a clot. Where large skin surface is involved, the threat of infection may be more serious than the loss of blood (figure 4.07).

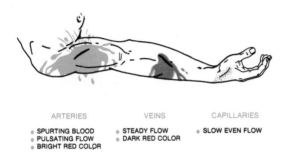

ARTERIES	VEINS	CAPILLARIES
• SPURTING BLOOD	• STEADY FLOW	• SLOW EVEN FLOW
• PULSATING FLOW	• DARK RED COLOR	
• BRIGHT RED COLOR		

FIGURE 4.07.—Bleeding characteristics.

"Bleeders"

Some persons' blood will not clot. Such people are hemophiliacs, commonly called "bleeders." They may bleed to death even from the slightest wounds where blood vessels are cut. In addition to applying compress bandage or gauze, such persons should be rushed to the nearest hospital, where medical treatments may be quickly administered.

Methods of Controlling Bleeding

Bleeding control is often very simple. Most external bleeding can be controlled by applying direct pressure to the open wound. Direct pressure permits normal blood clotting to occur.

In cases of severe bleeding, the first aider may be upset by the appearance of the wound and the emotional state of the victim. It is important for the first aider to keep calm.

Direct Pressure

The best all around method of controlling bleeding is applying pressure directly to the wound. This is best done by placing gauze or the cleanest material available against the bleeding point and applying firm pressure with the hand until a bandage can be applied. The bandage knot should be tied over the wound unless otherwise indicated. The bandage supplies direct pressure and should not be removed until the victim is examined by a physician. When air splints or pressure bandages are available, they may be used over the heavy layer of gauze to supply direct pressure (figure 4.08).

If bleeding continues after the bandage has been put on, this indicates that not enough pressure has been applied. Use the hand to put more pressure on the wound through the gauze, or tighten the bandage. Either method should control the bleeding. In severe bleeding, if gauze or other suitable material is not available, the bare hand should be used to apply direct pressure immediately.

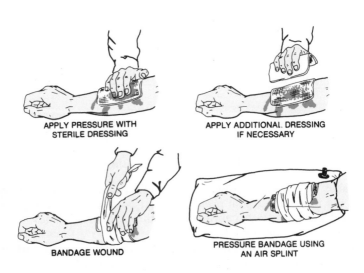

APPLY PRESSURE WITH STERILE DRESSING

APPLY ADDITIONAL DRESSING IF NECESSARY

BANDAGE WOUND

PRESSURE BANDAGE USING AN AIR SPLINT

FIGURE 4.08.—Direct pressure.

Elevation

Elevating the bleeding part of the body above the level of the heart will slow the flow of blood and speed clotting. Elevation should be used together with direct pressure when there are no unsplintable fractures and it will cause no pain or aggravation to the injury.

Indirect Pressure

Arterial bleeding can be controlled by digital thumb or finger pressure applied at pressure points. Pressure points are places over a bone where arteries are close to the skin. Pressing the artery against the underlying bone can control the flow of blood to the injury. There are 26 pressure points on the body—13 on each side—situated along main arteries (figure 4.09).

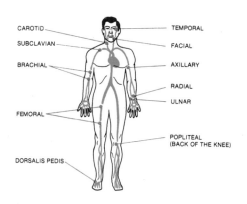

CAROTID

SUBCLAVIAN

BRACHIAL

FEMORAL

DORSALIS PEDIS

TEMPORAL

FACIAL

AXILLARY

RADIAL

ULNAR

POPLITEAL
(BACK OF THE KNEE)

FIGURE 4.09.—Pressure points.

In cases of severe bleeding where direct pressure is not controlling the bleeding, digital pressure must be used. Pressure points should be used with caution, as indirect pressure may cause damage to the limb as a result of an inadequate flow of blood. When the use of indirect pressure at a pressure point is necessary, indirect pressure should not be substituted for direct pressure; both kinds of pressure should be used. The pressure point should be held only as long as necessary to stop the bleeding. Indirect pressure should be reapplied if bleeding recurs.

Pressure points on the arms (brachial pressure point) and in the groin (femoral pressure point) are the ones most often used in first aid. These pressure points should be throughly understood.

Pressure on the brachial artery is used to control severe bleeding from an open wound on the upper extremity. This pressure point is located in a groove on the inside of the arm and the elbow. To apply pressure, grasp the middle of the victim's arm with the thumb on the outside of the arm and the fingers on the inside. Press the fingers toward the thumb. Use the flat, inside surface of the fingers, not the fingertips. This inward pressure closes the artery by pressing it against the arm bone (figure 4.10).

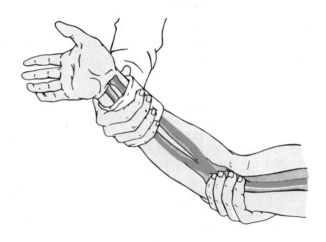

FIGURE 4.10.—Brachial pressure point.

The femoral artery is used to control severe bleeding from a wound on the lower extremity. The pressure point is located on the front, center part of the crease in the groin area. This is where the artery crosses the pelvic basin on the way into the lower extremity. To apply pressure, position the victim flat on his or her back, if possible. Kneeling on the opposite side from the wounded limb, place the heel of one hand directly on the pressure point and lean forward to apply the small amount of pressure needed to close the artery (figure 4.11). If bleeding is not controlled, it may be necessary to press directly over the artery with the flat surface of the fingertips and apply additional pressure on the fingertips with the heel of the other hand.

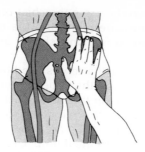

FIGURE 4.11.—Femoral pressure point.

Tourniquets

A tourniquet is a device used to control severe bleeding. It is used as a *last resort* after all other methods have failed. First-aiders should thoroughly understand the dangers and limitations of its use.

A tourniquet should normally be used only for severe, life-threatening hemorrhage that cannot be controlled by other means. A tourniquet may be dangerous. Its improper use by inexperienced, untrained persons may cause tissue injury. It may completely shut off the entire blood supply to a limb, and the pressure device itself often cuts into or injures the skin and underlying tissue. It is only rarely required and should be used only when large arteries are severed or in cases of partial or complete severance of a limb part, and when bleeding is uncontrollable.

With the fall in blood pressure and the unusual amount of blood that goes to fill the dilated blood vessels within the body, less blood returns to the heart for recirculation. In an effort to overcome the decreased volume and still send blood to all parts of the body, the heart pumps faster but pumps a much lower quantity of blood per beat. Thus, pulse is rapid and weak.

The blood suffers from this decreased blood supply and does not function normally; the victim's powers of reasoning, thinking, and expression are dulled.

The standard tourniquet usually is a piece of web belting about 36 inches long, with a buckle or snap device to hold it tightly in place when applied. A tourniquet can be improvised from a strap, belt, suspender, handkerchief, towel, necktie, cloth, or other suitable material. A tourniquet should be at least two inches wide to distribute pressure over tissues. Never use wire, cord, or anything that will cut into the flesh. A cravat bandage may be used as a tourniquet (figure 4.12).

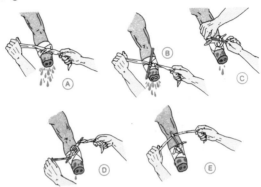

FIGURE 4.12.—Applying a tourniquet.

The procedure for application of a tourniquet is as follows:

- While the proper pressure point is being held to temporarily control the bleeding, place the tourniquet between the heart and wound, with sufficient uninjured flesh between the wound and tourniquet.

- In using an improvised tourniquet, wrap the material tightly around the limb twice and tie in a half knot on the upper surface of the limb (A of figure 4.12).

- Place a short stick or similar stout object at the half knot and tie a full knot (B of figure 4.12).

- Twist the stick to tighten the tourniquet only until the bleeding stops (C of figure 4.12).

- Secure the stick in place with the base ends of the tourniquet, another strip of cloth or suitable material (D & E of figure 4.12).

- Do not cover a tourniquet.

- Make a written note of the tourniquet's location and the time it was applied and attach the note to the victim's clothing. Alternatively, make a "T" on the victim's forehead.

- Get the victim to a medical facility as soon as possible.

Once the tourniquet is tightened, it should not be loosened except by or on the advice of a doctor. The loosening of a tourniquet may dislodge clots and result in sufficient loss of blood to cause severe shock and death.

A deep wound high up on the arm or an amputation at the upper part of the arm may require a tourniquet at the armpit to control bleeding. If needed, apply as follows:

- Place the center of a narrow cravat bandage in the armpit over a firm pad or padded object.

- Cross the ends on shoulder over a pad.

- Carry the ends around the back and chest to the opposite side and tie them over the pad.

- To tighten, insert a small stick or similar object under the cross of the bandage on the shoulder and twist. Twist only until the bleeding is controlled. Then secure or anchor the stick to prevent untwisting (figure 4.13).

- Loosen the tourniquet only on a doctor's advice.

FIGURE 4.13.—Tourniquet at armpit.

Internal Bleeding

Internal bleeding in the chest or abdominal cavities generally results from hard blows or certain fractures. Internal bleeding is usually not visible, but it can be very serious, even fatal. Internal bleeding may be determined by the following signs and symptoms (figure 4.14).

FIGURE 4.14.—Internal bleeding.

—Pain, tenderness, or discoloration where injury is suspected.

—Bleeding from mouth, rectum, or other natural bodying openings.

—Dizziness, without other symptoms. Dizziness when going from lying to standing may be the only early sign of internal bleeding.

—Cold and clammy skin.

—Eyes dull, vision clouded, and pupils enlarged.

—Weak and rapid pulse.

—Nausea and vomiting.

—Shallow and rapid breathing.

—Thirst.

—Weak and helpless feeling.

Emergency care for internal bleeding is to secure and maintain an open airway and treat for shock. Never give the victim anything by mouth.

Anyone suspected of having any internal bleeding should be transported to professional medical help as quickly and safely as possible. When blood or vomit is coming from the mouth, the injured person should be kept on his or her side. For chest injuries, place the victim on the injured side. Transport the victim gently and allow the victim to breathe oxygen if it is available.

If the internal bleeding is into an extremity, apply pressure to the injured place with a snug bandage or an air splint over a heavy pad. Elevate the part after it has been immobilized. Pressure will tend to close off the ends of the bleeding vessels. If it is possible that a closed fracture has caused the bleeding, care must be taken in applying any pressure dressing. Application directly over the fracture site might further injure tissue or complicate the fracture.

Nosebleeds

Nosebleeds are relatively common source of emergencies. They can result from injury, disease, activity, the environment and other causes. Generally, they are more annoying than serious, but enough blood may be lost to cause a slight degree of shock. Bleeding from the nose can be caused by the following:

—Facial injuries, including those caused by a direct blow to the nose.

—A cold, sinusitis, infections, or other abnormalities of the inside of the nose.

—High blood pressure.

—Strenuous activity.

—Exposure to high altitudes.

—Fractured skull.

If a fractured skull is suspected as the cause of a nosebleed, do not attempt to stop the bleeding. To do so might increase the pressure on the brain. The victim should be treated for a fractured skull as explained in chapter 8.

Nosebleed from other causes may be treated as follows:

- Keep the victim quiet and in a sitting position, leaning forward. If the sitting position is not possible because of other injuries, place the victim in a reclining position with head and shoulders raised.

- Apply pressure by pinching the nostrils.

- Apply cold compresses to the nose and face.

- If this does not control the bleeding, insert a small clean pad of gauze into one or both nostrils and again apply pressure with the thumb and finger pinching the nostrils. A free end of the gauze must extend outside the nostril so the pad can be removed later.

- If the person is conscious, it may be helpful to apply pressure beneath the nostril above the upper lip.

- Instruct the victim to avoid blowing the nose for several hours, as this could dislodge the clot.

- If bleeding continues, obtain medical assistance.

CHAPTER 5. SHOCK

The term "shock" has a number of meanings. In this chapter "shock" means a collapse or depression of the cardiovascular system due to an accident or sudden illness. Shock interferes with the normal action of the heart, respiration, and circulation and may result from a variety of causes.

The nervous system plays an important role in shock. The various parts of the body and the organs controlling the body functions are coordinated by the nervous system. This system consists of two separate but interconnected and coordinated systems: the cerebrospinal and the sympathetic (figure 5.01).

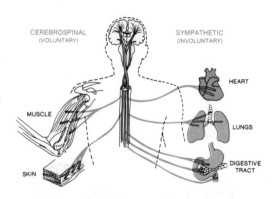

FIGURE 5.01.—Cerebrospinal and sympathetic nervous system.

The cerebrospinal system consists of the brain and spinal cord. The brain is a collection of nerve centers. Leaving the brain, the nerves are bundled into the spinal cord, which passes down through the opening in the center of the backbone or spinal column and branches off to all parts and organs of the body.

The nerves entering and leaving the spinal cord are mainly of two types: sensory nerves, which convey sensations such as heat, cold, pain, and touch from different parts of the body to the brain; and motor nerves, which convey impulses from the brain to the muscles causing movement.

The sympathetic system is a series of nerve centers in the chest and abdominal cavity along the spinal column. Each of these nerve centers, although interconnected with the cerebral spinal system, presides over and controls vital organs and vital functions. This system is not under control of the will; rather through it involuntary muscles are stimulated to function without regard to our state of consciousness.

The cardiovascular system, as presented in chapter 4, is that system which circulates blood to all cells. Food and oxygen are transported to each part of the body and waste products are removed through this system.

The cardiovascular system is made up of tubes, called vessels; liquid contents, called blood; and the pump which is the heart. These vessels are able to dilate and constrict. The size of the vessels is changed by signals transmitted through nerve pathways from the nervous system to the muscles in the blood vessel walls.

When the body is in its normal state there is enough blood to fill the system completely—approximately 10 to 12 pints. The pumping action of the heart supplies all parts of the body with blood.

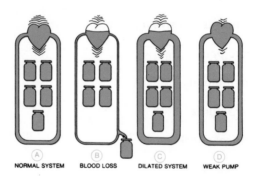

FIGURE 5.02.—Collapse of the cardiovascular system.

Shock is the failure of this system to provide sufficient circulation of blood to every part of the body.

The collapse of the cardiovascular system may be caused by any of three conditions:

1. Blood is lost (B of figure 5.02).

2. Vessels dilate and there is insufficient blood to fill them (C of figure 5.02).

3. The heart fails to act properly as a pump and circulate the blood (D of figure 5.02).

No matter what the reason for the collapse is, the results are the same: insufficient blood flow to provide nourishment and oxygen to all parts of the body. Because the body process may slow down, circulation is reduced and organs begin to die without nourishment.

Causes of Shock

The state of shock may develop rapidly or may be delayed until hours after the event that causes it. Shock occurs to some degree after every injury. It may be so slight as not to be noticed; or so serious that it results in death where the injuries received ordinarily would not prove fatal.

Some of the major causes of shock are as follows:

—Severe or extensive injuries.

—Severe pain.

—Loss of blood.

—Severe burns.

—Electrical shock.

—Gas poisoning.

—Certain illnesses.

—Allergic reactions.

—Bites or stings of poisonous snakes or insects.

—Poisons taken internally.

—Exposures to extremes of heat and cold.

—Emotional stress.

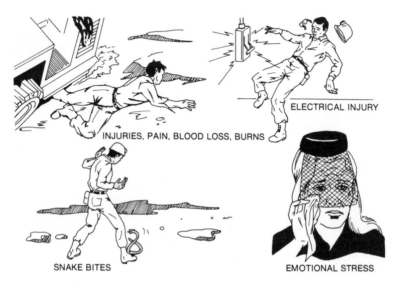

FIGURE 5.03.—Causes of shock.

Signs and Symptoms

The signs and symptoms of shock are both physical and emotional. The first aider should become familiar with these (figure 5.04).

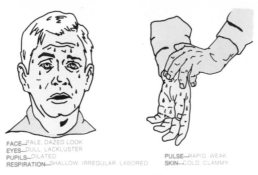

FACE—PALE, DAZED LOOK
EYES—DULL, LACKLUSTER
PUPILS—DILATED
RESPIRATION—SHALLOW, IRREGULAR, LABORED

PULSE—RAPID, WEAK
SKIN—COLD, CLAMMY

PERSON MAY BE PARTIALLY OR TOTALLY UNCONCIOUS, DISORIENTED

FIGURE 5.04.—Signs and symptoms of shock.

Some of the reactions known to take place within the body in cases of shock bear directly on the symptoms presented. The most important reaction that occurs in shock is a decided drop in normal blood flow, believed to be caused by involuntary nervous system losing control over certain small blood vessels. This is one of the reasons the victim is nauseous. The removal of blood from general circulation causes the blood pressure to fall, decreases the volume of blood passing through heart and lungs, and causes the vessels to dilate.

As a large amount of blood fills the dilated vessels within the body, the circulation near the surface is decreased, causing the skin to become pale, cold, and clammy. Other areas suffer as a result of the drop in circulation; the eyes are dull and lackluster and pupils may be dilated.

With the fall in blood pressure and the unusual amount of blood that goes to fill the dilated blood vessels within the body, less blood returns to the heart for recirculation. In an effort to overcome the decreased volume and still send blood to all parts of the body, the heart pumps faster but pumps a much lower quantity of blood per beat. Thus, pulse is rapid and weak.

The blood suffers from this decreased blood supply and does not function normally; the victim's powers of reasoning, thinking, and expression are dulled.

First Aid Care

Shock is a serious condition, but it is not irreversible if it is recognized quickly and treated effectively. Proper first aid care means caring for the whole victim, not just one or two of the victim's problems.

First aid care for the victim of physical shock is as follows:

- Keep the person lying down. Make sure that the head is at least level with the body, if the person is on the ground. Elevate the lower extremities if the injury will not be aggravated and there are no abdominal or head injuries. It may be necessary to raise the head and shoulders if a person is suffering from a head injury, sunstroke, apoplexy, heart attack or shortness of breath due to a chest or throat injury. However, it should be noted that if an accident was severe enough to produce a head injury there may also be spinal damage. If in doubt keep the victim flat.

- Control for bleeding.

- Always assure adequate breathing, as in all emergencies. If the victim is breathing, maintain an open airway. If the victim is not breathing, start artificial ventilation, or CPR if necessary (see chapter 12).

- Remove all foreign bodies from the victim's mouth, such as loose false teeth, tobacco, or gum, and cleanse the mouth of mucus or phlegm.

- Permit the victim to have plenty of fresh air. If possible administer oxygen. Oxygen deficiency results from the poor circulation, in cases of shock.

- Loosen tight clothing at the neck, chest, and waist, in order to make breathing and circulation easier.

- Handle the victim as gently as possible, and minimize movement.

- Keep the victim warm and dry by wrapping in blankets, clothing, brattice cloth, or other available material. These coverings should be placed under as well as over the victim to reduce the loss of body heat. Keep the victim warm enough to be comfortable. The objective is to maintain as near normal body temperature as possible not to add heat.

- The victim should not be given anything by mouth.

- The victim's emotional well-being is just as important as his or her physical well-being. Calm and reassure the victim. Never talk to the victim about his or her injuries. Keep onlookers away from the victim as their conversation regarding the victim's injuries may be upsetting.

Anaphylactic Shock

Various technical terms describe different types of shock. At least one of these, anaphylactic shock, should be given special emphasis because it does represent a true emergency.

Anaphylactic shock is a sensitivity reaction. It occurs when a person contacts something to which he or she is extremely allergic. People who are subject to anaphylactic shock should carry emergency medical identification at all times.

A person can contact substances which can cause anaphylactic shock by swallowing items such as fish or shellfish, berries, or oral drugs such as penicillin. Insect stings—those of yellow jackets, bees, wasps, hornets—or injected drugs can cause a violent reaction. So can inhaled substances such as dust or pollen.

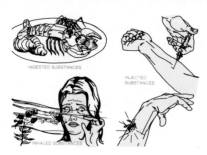

FIGURE 5.05.—Causes of anaphylactic shock.

Sensitivity reactions can occur within a few seconds after contact with the substance. Death can result within minutes of contact. Therefore, it is important that the person administering first aid care be able to recognize the signs and symptoms of anaphylactic shock:

—Itching or burning skin.

—Hives covering a large area.

—Swelling of the tongue and face.

—Difficulty in breathing.

—Tightening or pain in the chest.

—Weak pulse.

—Dizziness.

—Convulsion.

—Coma.

Anaphylactic shock is a true emergency and requires medication to counteract the allergic reaction. If the victim carries any medication, adrenalin or antihistamine, to counteract the allergy, the first aider should help the victim take the medicine.

The person should be transported to the hospital as quickly as possible because anaphylactic shock can be fatal in less than 15 minutes. Notify the hospital as to what caused the reaction; if known. Maintain an open airway. If necessary, provide artificial ventilation and CPR (see chapter 12) and treat for physical shock.

Fainting

Fainting is a temporary loss of consciousness due to an inadequate supply of oxygen to the brain and is a mild form of shock. Fainting may be caused by the sight of blood, exhaustion, weakness, heat, lack of air, or strong emotions such as fright or joy. Some people faint more easily than others.

The signs and symptoms of fainting are as follows:

—The victim may feel weak and dizzy, and may see black spots before his or her eyes.

—The face becomes pale and the lips blue.

—The forehead is covered with cold perspiration.

—The pulse is rapid and weak.

—The breathing is shallow.

The first aid care for fainting is as follows:

• The victim should lie down with the head lower than the feet or sit with the head between the knees.

• If the victim is unconscious for more than a short time, something may be seriously wrong. The victim should be taken to a medical facility as quickly as possible.

• Treat the victim for physical shock.

• Maintain an open airway.

FIGURE 5.06.—First aid care for fainting.

CHAPTER 6. WOUNDS AND DRESSINGS

Open Wounds

An open wound is any break in the skin. When the skin is unbroken, it afords protection from most bacteria or germs. However, germs may enter through even a small break in the skin, and an infection may develop. Any open wound should receive prompt medical attention. If germs have been carried into an open wound by the object causing the break in the skin, the flow of blood will sometimes wash out the germs; but, as will be explained later, some types of wounds do not bleed freely.

Breaks in the skin range from pin punctures of scratches to extensive cuts, tears, or gashes. An open wound may be the only surface evidence of a more serious injury such as a fracture, particularly in the case of head injuries involving fracture of the skull. In first aid, open wounds are divided into five classifications: abrasions, avulsions, incisions, lacerations, and punctures (figure 6.01).

Abrasions

Abrasions are caused by rubbing or scraping. These wounds are seldom deep, but a portion of the skin has been removed, leaving a raw, bleeding surface. The bleeding in most abrasions is from the capillaries. Abrasions are easily infected in proportion to the amount of underskin surface exposed.

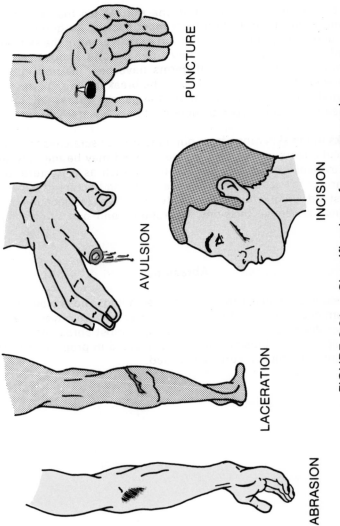

PUNCTURE

AVULSION

INCISION

LACERATION

ABRASION

FIGURE 6.01.—Classification of open wounds.

Avulsions

An avulsion is an injury that tears a whole piece of skin and tissue loose or leaves it hanging as a flap. This type of wound usually results when tissue is forcibly separated or torn from the victim's body. Body parts that have been wholly or partly torn off may sometimes be successfully re-attached by a surgeon.

Incisions

Wounds produced by a sharp cutting edge such as a knife, a piece of glass or metal, or a sharp edge of coal or rock are referred to as incised wounds. The edges of such wounds are smooth without bruising or tearing. If such a wound is deep, large blood vessels and nerves may be severed. Incised wounds bleed freely, and are often difficult to control.

Lacerations

Lacerated wounds are those with ragged edges. The flesh has been torn or mashed by blunt instruments, machinery, or rough surfaces. Because the blood vessels are torn or mashed. These wounds may not bleed as freely as incised wounds. The ragged and torn tissues, with the foreign matter that is often forced or ground into the wound, make the danger of infection greater than in incised wounds.

Punctures

Puncture wounds are produced by pointed instruments such as needles, splinters, nails, or pieces of wire. Such wounds usually are small in surface area, but they may be very deep. Often, the articles causing puncture wounds are soiled, and may cause infection. The small openings in puncture wounds and the small number of blood vessels cut can prevent free bleeding. The danger of infection in puncture wounds is far greater than in any other type of open wound because of this poor drainage.

General First Aid Care for Open Wounds

The chief duties of a first aider in caring for an open wound are to stop bleeding and to prevent germs from entering the wound. If germs do not enter, there will be much less chance of infection and the wound will heal quickly.

- Where there is severe bleeding from an artery, always check it by direct pressure and evaluation, and then, only if necessary, by the use of a tourniquet (A of figure 6.02).

- If a limb is involved, elevation will help to control bleeding.

- Shock usually follows wounds, especially if much blood is lost. Treat for shock promptly.

- Carefully cut or tear the clothing so that the injury may be seen.

- If loose foreign particles are around the wound, wipe them away with clean material. Always wipe away from the wound, not towards it.

- Do not attempt to remove a foreign object embedded in the wound, since it may aid the doctor in determining the extent of the injury. Serious bleeding and other damage may occur if the object is removed. Stabalize the object with a bulky dressing.

- Leave the work of cleansing the wound to the doctor. Antiseptics may be used by first aiders only when a physician supplies the items, gives instructions, and assumes responsibility for their use.

- Do not touch the wound with your hands, clothing, or anything that is not clean, if possible, and do not pour water or any other liquid into or on the wound.

- Place a bandage compress or gauze over the wound, and tie in place.

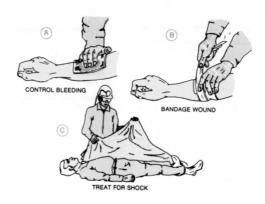

CONTROL BLEEDING

BANDAGE WOUND

TREAT FOR SHOCK

FIGURE 6.02.—First aid for open wounds.

- All dressings should be wide enough to completely cover the wound and the area around it.

- Protect all bandages, compresses, or gauze dressings by an outer dressing made from a cravat or triangular bandage, except dressings for wounds of the eye, nose, chin, finger, and toe, or compound fractures of the hand and foot when splints are applied. If the cravat bandage is already folded, open it enough to cover the entire dressing.

- Unless otherwise specified, tie the knots of the bandage compress and cover bandage over the wound on top of the compress pad to help in checking the bleeding.

First Aid Dressings and Bandages

First aid materials include triangular bandages that can be used either open or folded, strips of cloth, bandage compresses, gauze, roller bandages, trauma packs, tourniquets, and slings (figure 6.03).

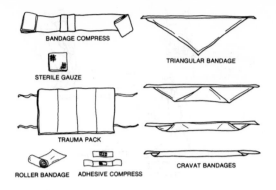

FIGURE 6.03.—Dressings and bandages.

Bandage Compress

A bandage compress is a special dressing to cover open wounds. It consists of a pad made of several thicknesses of gauze attached to the middle of a strip of gauze. Pad sizes range from 1 to 4 inches. Bandage compresses usually come folded so that the gauze pad can be applied directly to the open wound with virtually no exposure to the air or fingers. The strip of gauze at either side of the gauze pad is folded back so that it can be opened up and the bandage compress tied in place with no disturbance of the sterile pad. The gauze of a bandage compress may be extended to twice its normal size by opening up folded gauze. Unless otherwise specified, all bandage compresses and all gauze dressings should be covered with open triangular, cravat, or roller bandages.

Gauze

Gauze is used several ways in applying first aid dressings; plain gauze may be used in place of a bandage compress to cover large wounds. Plain gauze of various sizes is supplied in packets. Care should be taken not to touch the portion of the gauze that is to be placed in contact with the wound.

Special Pads

Large, thick-layered, bulky pads (some with an outer wa-
terproofed surface) are available in several sizes for quick application to an extremity or to a large area of the trunk. They are
used where bulk is required in cases of profuse bleeding. They
are also useful for stabilizing embedded objects. These special
pads are referred to as multi-trauma dressings, trauma packs,
general purpose dressings, or burn pads.

Because of their absorbent properties, sanitary napkins are well
suited for emergency care work. Being separately wrapped, they
insure a clean surface.

Triangular Bandages

A standard triangular bandage is made from a piece of cloth approximately 40 inches square by folding the square diagonally
and cutting along the fold. It is easily applied and can be handled
so that the part to be applied over wound or burn dressings will
not be soiled. A triangular bandage does not tend to slip off once
it is correctly applied. It is usually made from unbleached cotton
cloth, although any kind of cloth will do. In emergencies, a triangular bandage can be improvised from a clean handkerchief or
clean piece of shirt.

The triangular bandage is used to make improvised tourniquets,
to support fractures and dislocations, to apply splints, and to
form slings. If a regular-size bandage is found to be too short
when a dressing is applied, it can be lengthened by tying a piece
of another bandage to one end.

Cravat Bandages

A triangular bandage may be used open or folded. When folded it
is known as a cravat. A cravat bandage is prepared as follows:

- Make a 1 inch fold along the base of the triangular bandage.

- Bring the point to the center of the folded base, placing the point underneath the fold, this makes a wide cravat bandage.

- A medium cravat is made by folding lengthwise along a line midway between the base and the new top of the bandage.

- A narrow cravat is made if folding is repeated.

This method has the advantage that all bandages can be folded to a uniform width, or the width may be varied to suit the purpose for which it is to be used. To complete a dressing, the ends of the bandage are tied securely.

Square Knot

Unless otherwise specified, all knots or ties mentioned in this manual should be tied in a square knot because this knot can be easily loosened (figure 6.04).

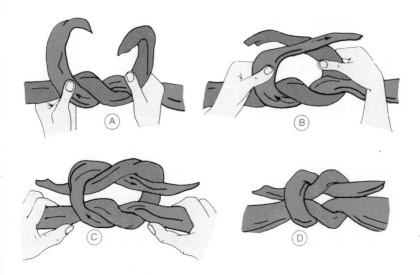

FIGURE 6.04.—Square knot.

| (A) | (B) | (C) |
| TRIANGLE SLING | CRAVAT SLING | BASKET SLING |

FIGURE 6.05.—Slings.

Slings

Slings are used to support injuries of the shoulder, upper extremities, or ribs. In an emergency they may be improvised from belts, neckties, scarves, or similar articles. Bandages should be used if available.

Triangular Bandage Sling

Tie a triangular bandage sling as follows:

- Place one end of the base of an open triangular bandage over the shoulder of the injured side.

- Allow the bandage to hang down in front of the chest so that the apex will be behind the elbow of the injured arm.

- Bend the arm at the elbow with hand slightly elevated (4 to 5 inches).

- Bring the forearm across the chest and over the bandage.

- Carry the lower end of the bandage over the shoulder of the uninjured side and tie at uninjured side of the neck, being sure the knot is at the side of the neck.

- Twist the apex of the bandage, and tuck it in at the elbow.

The hand should be supported with the fingertips exposed, whenever possible, to permit detection of interference with circulation (A of figure 6.05).

Cravat Bandage Sling

Tie a cravat bandage sling as follows:

- Place one end over the shoulder of the injured side.

- Allow the bandage to hang down in front of the chest.

- Bend the arm at the elbow with hand slightly elevated (4 to 5 inches).

- Bring the forearm across the chest and over the bandage.

- Carry the lower end of the bandage over the injured arm to the shoulder of the uninjured side and tie at uninjured side of neck (B of figure 6.05).

Basket Sling

A useful sling for transporting or handling an unconscious victim whose arms may create difficulties in handling, can be made with an open triangular bandage as follows:

- Place an open triangular bandage across the chest with the apex down.

- Fold the arms over one another on the bandage.

- Bring the ends together and tie.

- Cross the apex over the folded arms and tie to the knotted ends of the base (C of figure 6.05).

Principles of Bandaging

- Bandage wounds snugly, but not too tightly. Too tight a bandage may interfere with the blood supply and damage surrounding tissue.

- In bandaging the arms or the legs, leave the tips of the fingers or toes uncovered where possible so any interference with circulation can be detected.

- Always place the body part to be bandaged in the position in which it is to be left. Because swelling frequently follows an injury, a tight bandage may cause serious interference with circulation. On the other hand, a loosely applied bandage may slip off and expose the wound.

- If the victim complains the bandage is too tight, loosen it and make it comfortable but snug. Unless otherwise specified, all knots should be tied over open wounds to help control bleeding.

Dressings for Open Wounds

Scalp, Temple, Ear, or Face

To dress an open wound for the scalp, temple, ear, or face, proceed as follows:

- Apply the pad of a bandage compress over the wound.

- Carry one end under the chin, and the other over the top of the head.

- Cross at the temple in front of the ear on the side opposite the injury.

- Carry one end around the front of the head and the other end low around the back of the head.

- Tie on or near the compress pad.

- Cover the compress with a cravat bandage applied in the same manner (A and B of figure 6.06).

If the wound is on the cheek or the front of the face, cross the bandage compress and cravat bandage behind the ear, on the side opposite the injury; bring the ends around the forehead and back of the head, and tie (C of figure 6.06).

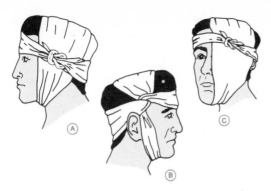

FIGURE 6.06.—Dressing for open wounds of the scalp, temple, ear, or face.

Extensive Wounds of the Scalp

A wound or wounds involving a large area of the scalp may be dressed by covering the injury with a piece of gauze or a large bandage compress.

- Carry one end under the chin and the other end over the top of the head.

- Cross the ends at the temple.

- Carry one end around the forehead.

- Pass the other end around the back of the head and tie on the opposite side of the face.

- Then apply a triangular bandage over the head with the base snugly across the forehead just above the eyebrows and the apex of the bandage at the back of the neck.

- Bring the two ends of the bandage around the head just above the ears.

- Cross under the bony prominence on the back of the head.

- Return the end to the middle of the forehead.

- Tie just above the eyebrows.

- Fold up the apex and tuck it in snugly over the crossed ends at the back of the head (figure 6.07).

When gauze is used, take care to keep it in place while the cover bandage is being applied.

FIGURE 6.07.—Dressing for extensive wound of the scalp.

Eye Injuries

Objects embedded in the eye should be removed only by a doctor. Such objects must be protected from accidental movement or removal until the victim receives medical attention.

- Tell the victim that both eyes must be bandaged to protect the injured eye.

- Encircle the eye with a gauze dressing or other suitable material.

- Position a crushed cup or cone over the embedded object. The object should not touch the top or sides of the cup (figure 6.08).

- Hold the cup and dressing in place with a bandage compress or roller bandage that covers both eyes. It is im-

82.

portant to bandage both eyes to prevent movement of the injured eye.

- Never leave the victim alone, as the victim may panic with both eyes covered. Keep in hand contact so the victim will always know someone is there.

- Stabilize the head with sand bags or large pads and always transport the victim on his or her back.

This procedure should also be used for lacerations and other injuries to the eyeball.

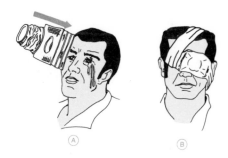

FIGURE 6.08.—Dressing for an embedded object in the eye.

After a serious injury, the eyeball may be knocked out of the socket. No attempt should be made to put the eye back into the socket. The eye should be covered with a moist dressing and a protective cup without applying pressure to the eye. A bandage compress or roller bandage that covers both eyes should be applied. Transport the victim face up with the head immobilized.

For all injuries to the area around the upper or lower lid of the eye, use a sterile bandage compress as follows:

- Place the center of a bandage compress over the injured eye.

- Carry the other end above the ear on the opposite side.

83

- Tie somewhat toward the injured side below the bony prominence on the back of the head.

- Bring both ends over the top of the head, passing the longer end under the dressing at the temple on the un-injured side.

- Slide it in front of the uninjured eye and pull it tightly enough to raise the dressing above the uninjured eye.

- Tie to the other end on top of the head (figure 6.09).

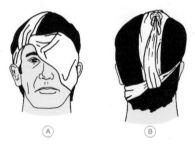

FIGURE 6.09.—Dressing for an injured eye.

Nose

To bandage a wound of the nose, proceed as follows:

- Split the tails of a bandage compress.

- Apply the pad of the compress to the wound.

- Pass the top tails, one to each side of the head below the ears and tie at back of neck.

- Pass the bottom tails, one to each side of the head above the ears and tie at the back of the head (A of figure 6.10).

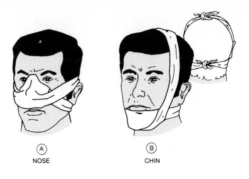

FIGURE 6.10.—Dressing for nose and chin.

Chin

In order to tie a bandage for a wound of the chin, proceed as follows:

- Split the tails of a bandage compress.

- Apply the pad of the compress to the wound.

- Pass the top tails, one to each side of the neck below the ears and tie at the back of the neck.

- Pass the bottom tails, one to each side of the head in front of the ears and tie at the top of the head (B of figure 6.10).

Shoulder

In order to tie a bandage for a wound of the shoulder, proceed as follows:

- Apply the pad of a bandage compress over the wound. Bring the ends under the armpit.

- Cross, carry to the top of the compress, cross, carry one end across the chest and one end across the back, and tie in the opposite armpit over a pad (A of figure 6.11).

- Place the apex of a triangular bandage high up on the shoulder: place the base, along which a hem has been folded, below the shoulder on the upper part of the arm; carry the ends around the arm and tie them on the outside.

- To hold the bandage in position, place the center of a cravat bandage under the opposite armpit; carry the ends to the shoulder over the apex; tie a single knot (B of figure 6.11); then fold the apex over and complete the knot.

- Place the forearm in a triangular bandage sling (C of figure 6.11).

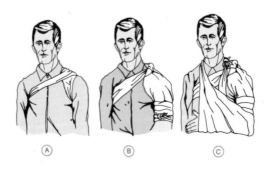

FIGURE 6.11.—Dressing for a wound of the shoulder.

Armpit

To dress a wound of the armpit, proceed as follows:

- Apply the pad of a bandage compress over the wound. Lift the arm only high enough to apply compress, as further damage may occur to lacerated nerves which are close to the surface.

- Carry one end across the chest and the other end across the back.

- Tie under the opposite arm over a pad (figure 6.12).

- If there is severe bleeding, place a firm pad over the pad of the compress and push it well up into the armpit, holding the pads in place by a cravat bandage. Bring the ends over the shoulder, crossing them. Then pass the ends around the chest and back and tie them under the opposite arm. Then bring the arm down and secure it firmly against the chest wall by a cravat bandage passed around the arm and chest. Tie securely on the opposite side over a pad.

- Place the forearm in a cravat bandage.

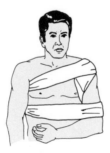

FIGURE 6.12.—Dressing for a wound of the armpit.

Amputations

Arm Torn From Body

When an arm has been torn from the body at the socket, there is profuse bleeding from the larger blood vessels that are severed; therefore, care must be prompt. The first aid care for an arm torn from the body is as follows:

- An assistant should apply pressure to the subclavian pressure point (see chapter 4 and figure 6.13) to help control hemorrhage temporarily.

- Reach into the wound and pinch the major blood vessels, if possible.

- Pack the wound with gauze. But if there is no gauze at hand, do not wait; place your fingers in the wound and pinch the blood vessels while an assistant obtains and prepares gauze. When it is ready, let go of the vessels and push the sterile gauze firmly into the wound.

- Apply the pad of a bandage compress over the seat of the injury, passing the ends around the chest and back, tying securely under the opposite arm over a pad.

- Then place the center of a suitable cravat bandage over the pad, carrying the ends across the chest and back.

- Tie under the opposite armpit.

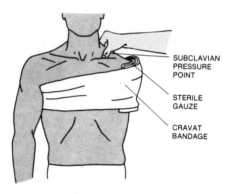

FIGURE 6.13.—Dressing for an arm torn from body.

Other Amputations

Care for the victim of an amputation, proceed as follows:

- Control hemorrhage by digital pressure until a tourniquet is applied.

- Dress the end of the stump with gauze.

- Place the stump in the center of a triangular bandage with the base against the inside of the extremity.

- Carry the apex over the stump and up on the outside of the extremity.

- Cross the ends on the outside of the extremity.

- Bring the ends around the limb and cross them under the limb.

- Bring the ends to the front of the limb and tie.

- Fold the apex over the knot and tuck it under (figure 6.14).

In cases of avulsions and amputations of extremities collect the separated parts, place them in a plastic bag, then in iced water (do not immerse the part in water directly), and transport to the medical facility.

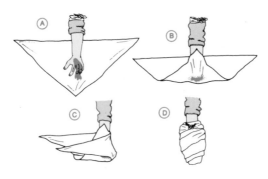

FIGURE 6.14.—Dressing for amputation.

Elbow or Knee

To dress a wound of the elbow or knee, proceed as follows:

- Start with the joint in a slightly bent position.

- Apply the pad of a bandage compress over the wound.

- Pass the ends of the bandage around the joint and cross them.

- Carry the ends around the limb just above the joint and cross them.

- Carry them around the limb just below the joint and cross them.

- Tie on the outer side (figure 6.15).

- Cover with a cravat bandage following the same procedure.

For an injury to the elbow, immobilize the upper extremity by putting the forearm in a sling or tying it to the body.

APPLY STERILE BANDAGE COMPRESS, COVER WITH CRAVAT BANDAGE

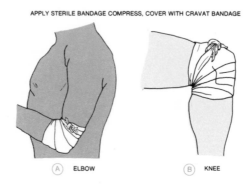

(A) ELBOW   (B) KNEE

FIGURE 6.15.—Dressing for the elbow or knee.

Palm or Back of the Hand

To dress a wound of the palm or back of the hand, proceed as follows:

- Apply the pad of a bandage compress over the wound.

- Pass the ends several times around the hand and wrist.

- Tie over the pad.

- Place the center of a cravat bandage over the pad.

- Cross the ends at the opposite side of the hand.

- Bring one end between the thumb and forefinger.

- Carry the other end around the little finger side, bringing the ends to the wrist.

- Cross the ends and continue around the wrist, crossing at the back of the wrist.

- Cross again at the inside of the wrist.

- Tie at the back of the wrist (figure 6.16).

- Place the forearm and hand in a triangular bandage sling.

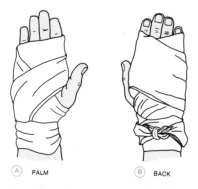

(A) PALM   (B) BACK

FIGURE 6.16.—Dressing for the palm or back of the hand.

Extensive Wounds of the Hand

To dress extensive wounds of the hand, proceed as follows:

- Apply gauze or a bandage compress over the wound.

- When there are multiple wounds of fingers, separate the fingers with gauze.

- If a bandage compress is used, pass the ends several times around the hand and wrist.

- Tie them over the pad.

Cover the hand with a triangular bandage as follows:

- Place the base on the inner side of the wrist.

- Bring the apex down over the back of the hand.

- Cross the ends over the back of the hand and wrist.

- Cross the ends on the inside of the wrist.

- Bring the ends of the bandage to the back of the wrist and tie.

- Bring the apex down over the knot and tuck it under (figure 6.18).

- Place the forearm and hand in a triangular bandage sling.

- If there is swelling and fracture, elevate and apply ice.

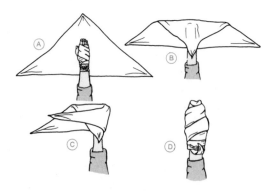

FIGURE 6.17.—Cover bandage for extensive wounds of the hand.

Finger

To dress a wound of the finger, proceed as follows:

- Apply the pad of a small bandage compress over the wound.

- Pass the ends several times around the finger.

- Tie the ends over the pad. A small adhesive compress for the finger may be used instead of a bandage compress. A bent finger should be dressed bent and not fully extended.

End of Finger

To dress a wound to the end of the finger, proceed as follows:

- Apply the pad of a small bandage compress over the wound so that the tails hang down on the front and back of the finger.

- Hold the tails securely in place at the base of the finger.

- Make one circular turn with one of the tails above that point to anchor the bandage.

- Carry this tail to the end of the finger.

- Make a circular turn around the base of the finger.

- Carry the tail by spiral turns to the starting point.

- Omitting the first circular turning, apply the other tail in a similar manner with spiral turns in the opposite direction.

- Tie the ends on the back of the finger (figure 6.18).

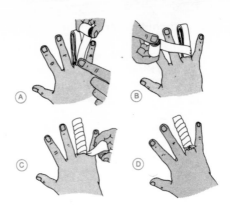

FIGURE 6.18.—Dressing for end of finger.

When the ends of two or more fingers are injured, proceed as follows:

- Apply a small adhesive bandage over the ends of each injured finger, or apply a small bandage compress to each finger following the same procedure described previously.

- Cover as for extensive wounds of the hand.

- Support the arm with a triangular bandage sling.

Chest or Back Between the Shoulders

To dress a wound high up on the chest or back, proceed as follows:

- Place the pad of the compress over the wound so that the ends are diagonally across the chest or back.

- Carry one end over the shoulder and under the opposite armpit. Carry the other end under the armpit and over the opposite shoulder. Tie the ends over the compress (A of figure 6.19).

94

Cover the compress and chest or back with a triangular bandage as follows:

- Place the center of the base at the lower part of the neck.

- Allow the apex to drop down over the chest or back, as appropriate.

- Carry the ends over the shoulders and under the armpits to the center of the chest.

- Tie with the apex below the knot.

- Turn the apex up and tuck it over the knot (B of figure 6.20).

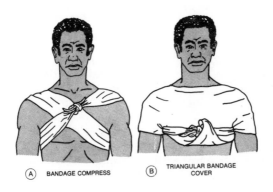

(A) BANDAGE COMPRESS   (B) TRIANGULAR BANDAGE COVER

FIGURE 6.19.—Dressing for a wound to the chest between the shoulders.

Protruding Intestine

To dress a wound in which the victim's intestines are protruding, proceed as follows:

- Do not try to replace the intestines; leave the organ on the surface.

- Cover with a moist dressing.

- Cover with an outer dressing.

Lower Part of Abdomen, Lower Back, or Buttocks

To dress a wound of the lower part of the abdomen, the lower part of the back or the buttocks, proceed as follows:

- Apply a pad made from several layers of sterile gauze; in the absence of gauze, the pad of a sterile compress may be placed over the wound and held in place by passing the ends around the body and tying them.

- Cover the gauze or bandage compress with two triangular bandages.

- Tie the apexes in the crotch.

- Bring the base of one bandage up on the abdomen.

- Pass the ends around to the back, and tie (figure 6.20).

- Pass the ends of the other bandage around to the front and tie (C of figure 6.20)

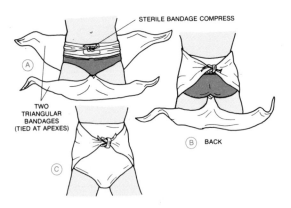

FIGURE 6.20.—Dressing for wounds of the abdomen, lower back or buttocks.

Groin

To dress a wound of the groin, proceed as follows:

- Apply the pad of a bandage compress over the wound.

- Carry the ends to the hip and cross.

- Carry the ends across to the opposite side of the body and tie (A of figure 6.21).

Cover the compress with two cravat bandages (tied together) as follows:

- Place the center of one of the cravat bandages over the pad and follow the compress in such a manner as to cover it entirely.

- Continuing with the cravat bandages, pass them around the entire body a second time and tie (B of figure 6.21).

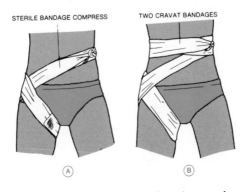

STERILE BANDAGE COMPRESS   TWO CRAVAT BANDAGES

(A)   (B)

FIGURE 6.21.—Dressing for the groin.

Hip

To dress a wound of the hip, proceed as follows:

- Split the tails of a bandage compress.

- Place the pad over the wound.

- Pass the top tails around the body.

- Tie over the opposite hip.

- Pass one end of the bottom tail around the front of the thigh and the other end over the buttock of the injured side, crossing below the crotch.

- Continue around the thigh, tying on the outside.

Cover with a triangular bandage as follows:

- Place the base on the thigh with the apex up and tie the ends of the base around the leg.

- Pass a cravat bandage around the body and tie a single knot over the apex.

- Fold the apex over the knot and complete tying the knot (B of figure 6.22).

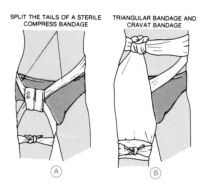

SPLIT THE TAILS OF A STERILE COMPRESS BANDAGE

TRIANGULAR BANDAGE AND CRAVAT BANDAGE

(A)   (B)

FIGURE 6.22.—Dressing for the hip.

Crotch

To dress a wound of the crotch, proceed as follows:

- Apply the pad of a bandage compress to the wound.

- Bring one end up between the buttocks and around the body over the hip to the center of the abdomen, passing over the other end.

- Fold the first end back in the direction from which it came; pass the other end around the body, in the opposite direction.

- Tie at the side of the hip.

- Pass a narrow cravat bandage around the waist and tie in front, leaving the ends to hang free.

- Pass a second cravat bandage under the knot of the first cravat bandage (A of figure 6.24).

- Pass the two ends of the second cravat bandage between the thighs and bring one end around each hip.

- Tie to the ends of the cravat bandage tied around the body (B of figure 6.23).

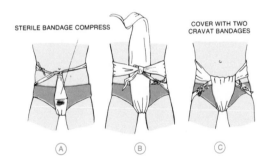

STERILE BANDAGE COMPRESS

COVER WITH TWO
CRAVAT BANDAGES

Ⓐ   Ⓑ   Ⓒ

FIGURE 6.23.—Dressing for the crotch.

Head, Body, and Extremities

Dressing for the forehead, back of the head, upper extremities (arm, forearm, and wrist), back, chest, abdomen, side and lower extremities (thigh and leg) can be made by applying a wraparound bandage as follows:

- Apply the pad of a bandage compress over the wound.

- Pass the ends around the injured part and tie over the pad. If the injury is to the trunk, carry one end across the back and the other end across the front and tie on the opposite side of the body.

- Place the center of a cravat bandage over the compress, pass the ends around the injured part, cross them, bring them around again, and tie over the pad. If the injury is to the trunk, place the center of the proper size cravat bandage over the injured side; take the ends across the back and front of body and tie on the opposite side (figure 6.24).

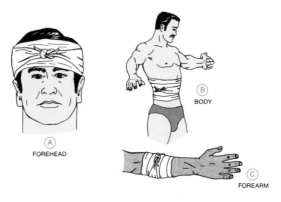

FIGURE 6.24.—Wraparound bandage.

Ankle

To dress a wound of the ankle, proceed as follows:

- Apply the pad of a bandage compress to the wound.

- Carry the ends around the ankle and cross over the instep.

- Carry around the bottom of the foot and cross over the instep again.

- Pass the ends around the ankle and tie over the pad.

- Place the center of a cravat bandage over the compress.

- Pass one end over the instep, under the bottom of the foot, and over the instep again.

- Take the other end around the ankle, over the compress, and around the ankle a second time.

- Bring the end crossing the instep around the back of the ankle above the heel.

- Tie the ends over the pad (figure 6.25).

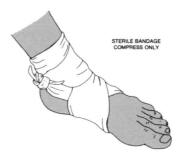

STERILE BANDAGE
COMPRESS ONLY

FIGURE 6.25.—Dressing for the ankle.

Foot

To dress a wound of the foot, proceed as follows:

- Apply the pad of a bandage compress to the wound.

- Carry the ends around the foot and ankle.

- Tie over the pad.

- Place the center of a cravat bandage over the compress.

- Carry the ends around the foot and ankle, ending in a tie as near the front of ankle as possible (figure 6.26).

FIGURE 6.26.—Dressing for a wound of the foot.

Extensive Wounds and Bleeding of Foot

Control arterial bleeding of the foot by digital pressure; then apply a tourniquet if necessary. A tourniquet, if required, should be applied over uninjured tissue, above the wound and as near it as possible.

Elevating the injured foot will also help decrease the blood flow.

To dress extensive wounds of the foot, proceed as follows:

- Apply gauze or the pad of a large bandage compress over the wound and tie it in place.

- Place the base of the bandage on the back of the ankle.

- Bring the apex under the sole of the foot, over the toes, back over the instep, and up the leg to a point above the ankle in front.

- Pass the end on the little toe side over the instep, then the other end over the instep, and continue around the ankle with both ends and tie in front.

- Bring the apex down over the knot and tuck in under the knot (figure 6.27).

FIGURE 6.27.—Dressing for extensive wounds of the foot.

Toe

To dress a wound of the toe, proceed as follows:

- Apply the pad of a small bandage compress over the wound.

- Pass the ends around the toe several times and tie over the pad.

If more than one toe is injured, apply a small bandage compress to each toe.

A small adhesive compress may be used instead of a bandage compress. If more than one toe is injured, apply a small adhesive compress to each toe. Once the toe or toes have been bandaged, they should be covered with a triangular bandage as described for extensive wounds and bleeding of the foot.

End of Toe

To dress a wound to the end of the toe, proceed as follows:

- Apply a small adhesive compress bandage, or apply the pad of a small bandage compress over the wound. When two or more toes are injured, apply a small bandage compress, or a small adhesive compress bandage, to each toe.

- Cover with an open triangular bandage as described for extensive wounds of the foot.

Closed Wounds

Closed wounds are injuries where the skin is not broken, but damage occurs to underlying tissues. These injuries may result in internal bleeding, damage to internal organs, and muscle and other tissue damage. Closed wounds are classified as follows:

—Bruises.

—Sprains.

—Strains.

—Ruptures or hernias.

Bruises

Bruises are caused by an object striking the body or the body coming into contact with a hard object, for example in a fall or a bump. The skin is not broken, but the soft tissues beneath the skin are damaged. Small blood vessels are ruptured, causing blood to seep into surrounding tissues. This produces swelling. The injured area appears red at first, then darkens to blue or purple. When large blood vessels have been ruptured or large amounts of underlying tissue have been damaged, a lump may develop as a result of the blood collecting within the damaged tissue. This lump is called a hematoma or blood tumor. The symptoms of a bruise are as follows:

—Immediate pain.

—Swelling.

—Rapid discoloration.

—Later pain or pressure on movement.

The first aid care for bruises is as follows:

- Apply cold applications to limit swelling and reduce pain by applying an ice bag, a cloth wrung out in cold water, or a chemical cold pack.

- Elevate the injured area and place at complete rest.

- Check for fractures and other possible injuries.

- Treat for shock.

- Severe bruises should have the care of a doctor.

Sprains

Sprains are injuries due to stretching or tearing ligaments or other tissues at a joint. They are caused by a sudden twist or stretch of a joint beyond its normal range of motion (figure 6.28).

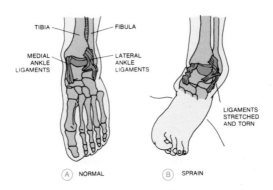

FIGURE 6.28.—Sprain.

Sprains may be minor injuries, causing pain and discomfort for only a few hours. In severe cases, however, they may require many weeks of medical care before normal use is restored.

The symptoms of a sprain are as follows:

—Pain on movement.

—Swelling.

—Tenderness.

—Discoloration.

Sprains present basically the same signs as a closed fracture, and for this reason *all* injuries to bones and joints should be immobilized.

The first aid care for sprains is as follows:

- Elevate the injured area and place it at complete rest.

- Reduce swelling and relieve pain by applying an ice bag, a cloth wrung in cold water or a chemical cold pack. (Remember, never put ice in direct contact with the skin; always wrap it in a towel or other material.)

- If swelling and pain persist, take the victim to the doctor.

The ankle is the part of the body most commonly affected by sprains. When the ankle has been sprained and the injured person must use the foot temporarily to reach a place for further care, the following care should be given:

- Unlace the shoe, but do not remove it.

- Place the center of a narrow cravat bandage under the foot in front of the heel of the shoe.

- Carry the ends up and back of the ankle, crossing above the heel, then forward, crossing over the instep, and then downward toward the arch to make a hitch under the cravat on each side, just in front of the heel of the shoe.

- Pull tight and carry the ends back across the instep.

- Tie at the back of the ankle (figure 6.29).

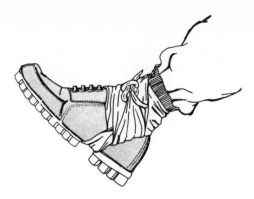

FIGURE 6.29.—Bandage for a sprained ankle.

Strains

A strain is an injury of a muscle or a tendon caused by overexertion. The muscle fibers are stretched and in severe cases the muscle or tendon may be torn. Strains are caused by sudden movements or overexertion.

The symptoms of a strain are as follows:

—Intense pain.

—Moderate swelling.

—Painful and difficult movement.

—In some cases, discoloration.

The first aid care for a strain is as follows:

• Place the victim in a comfortable position.

• Apply a hot, wet towel.

• Keep the injured area at rest.

• Seek medical attention.

Ruptures or Hernias

The most common form of rupture or hernia is a protrusion of a portion of an internal organ through the wall of the abdomen. Most ruptures occur in or just above the groin, but they may occur at other places over the abdomen. Ruptures result from a combination of weakness of the tissues and muscular strain.

The symptoms of a rupture are as follows:

- —Sharp, stinging pain.

- —Feeling of something giving way at the site of the rupture.

- —Swelling.

- —Possible nausea and vomiting.

The first aid care for an individual who has suffered a rupture is as follows:

- Lay the victim on his or her back with the knees well drawn up.

- Place the center of a cravat bandage on the outside of the thighs and pass the ends around the thighs, cross under the knees, bring the ends around the legs just above the ankles and tie.

- Place a blanket or similar padding under the knees.

- Never attempt to force the protrusion back into the cavity.

- Cover with a blanket.

- The victim should be transported in this position (figure 6.30).

FIGURE 6.30.—First aid for a rupture or hernia.

CHAPTER 7. BURNS

A burn is an injury that results from contact with heat, chemical agents, electricity, or radiation. Burns vary in depth, size, and degree of severity. The problems most often associated with burns are the following:

—Loss of body fluids contributing to shock.

—Pain contributing to shock.

—Anxiety contributing to shock.

—Swelling.

—Infection due to destruction of skin tissue.

—Airway or respiratory difficulties.

Classification of Burns

Burns may be classified according to cause. The four major types of burns by cause are as follows:

—Thermal.

—Chemical.

—Electrical.

—Radiation.

Burns may also be classified according to extent and depth of damage as follows:

—First degree   — The burned area is painful.
The outer skin is reddened.
Slight swelling is present.

—Second degree — The burned area is painful.
The underskin is affected.
Blisters may be formed.
The area may have a wet, shiny appearance because of exposed tissue.

—Third degree — Insensitive due to the destruction of nerve endings.
Skin is destroyed.
Muscle tissues and bone underneath may be damaged.
The area may be charred, white, or grayish in colór.

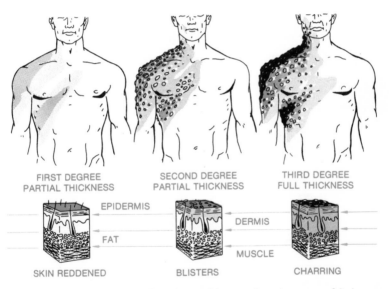

FIGURE 7.01.—Classification of burns by degree of injury.

Determining the Severity of Burns

The "Rule of Nines" can be used to quickly calculate the amount of skin surface that has received burns. Most areas of the adult body can be divided into portions of 9 percent or multiples of 9 percent (figure 7.02).

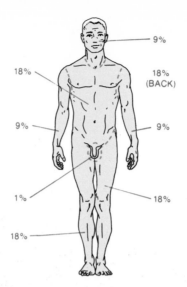

FIGURE 7.02.—Rule of Nines: adult percentages.

The hand can be used as a good reference, as it represents about one percent of the body. For determining the severity of burns in children and infants, the same percentages as used in adults may be used, with the exception of the head and legs (figure 7.03).

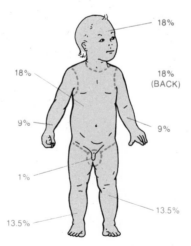

FIGURE 7.03.—Rule of Nines: child and infant percentages.

The severity of the burn can be determined when the degree of the burn and the amount of body surface burned have been determined. Burns are classified by severity: critical (severe), moderate, or minor.

Critical Burns

The following conditions constitute critical burns:

- —Second degree burns over more than 25 percent of the body.

- —Third degree burns over more than 10 percent of the body.

- —Third degree burns involving critical areas (face, hands, feet, or groin).

- —All burns complicated by respiratory problems, major wounds, or fractures.

- —All burns that encircle a joint, which may lead to loss of the joint's mobility.

Moderate Burns

The following conditions constitute moderate burns:

- —First degree burns involving most of the body.

- —Second degree burns between 15 percent to 25 percent of the body.

- —Third degree burns between 2 and 10 percent of the body (excluding face, hands, and feet).

Minor Burns

The following conditions constitute minor burns:

- —First degree burns.

—Second degree burns over less than 15 percent of the body.

—Third degree burns over less than 2 percent of the body. (excluding face, hands, and feet).

First Aid Care for Burns

The first aid care rendered to the burn victim largely depends on the cause of the burn and the degree of severity. Regardless of the severity of the burn, however, infection can be a serious problem. Certain principles need to be kept in mind when dealing with any burn victim:

- Remove the victim from burn source.

- Maintain airway and monitor respiration.

- Control any bleeding.

- Treat for shock and maintain body heat.

- When a burn and soft tissue wound are in the same area, treat as if a burn only.

- Remove clothing and loose debris, unless they are sticking to the burned surface.

- *Do not* try to clean the burn.

- Separate burned surfaces from contact with one another.

- Never use ointments, lotions or sprays unless recommended by a physician.

- Never use industrial grease or oil, butter, or similar cooking fats on burns.

- Don't break blisters.

- Splint fractures.

- If the victim can receive medical attention within one

hour, do not administer fluids orally, as this could induce vomiting.

- For the victim of critical or moderate burns, if competent medical help is not available for one hour or more and the victim is conscious and not vomiting, give the victim a weak solution of salt and soda (two pinches of salt and one pinch of baking soda to each 8 to 10-ounce glass of water).

- Recommend that victim check on tetanus immunization (needed every 5 years).

- Transport to a medical facility as soon as possible.

In addition to the general principles listed, certain other principles must be followed when giving first aid care for specific types of burns.

Thermal Burns (Minor)

General first aid care for minor thermal burns is as follows:

- Use cool, moist applications of gauze or bandage material to minimize blistering.

- Treat for physical shock.

Thermal Burns (Critical and Moderate)

General first aid care for more serious thermal burns is as follows:

- Do not use cold applications on extensive burns; cold could result in chilling.

- Cover the burn with a clean, dry dressing.

- Treat for shock.

- Transport to a medical facility.

Chemical Burns

General first aid care for chemical burns—not including alkali burns—is as follows:

- Remove all clothing containing the chemical agent.

- Do not use any neutralizing solution, unless recommended by a physician.

- Irrigate with water for at least 15 minutes, use potable water if possible.

- Treat for shock.

- Transport to a medical facility.

First aid care for alkali burns is an exception to the general first aid care for chemical burns because mixing water with dry alkali creates a corrosive substance. The dry alkali should be brushed from the skin and water should then be used in very large amounts.

Electrical Burns

General first aid care for electrical burns is as follows:

- Remove the victim from contact with electrical current, without coming into contact with the current yourself.

- Conduct a primary survey, as cardiac and respiratory arrest can occur in cases of electrical burns.

- Check for points of entry and exit of current.

- Cover burned surface with a clean dressing.

- Splint all fractures. (Violent muscle contractions caused by the electricity may result in fractures.)

- Treat for physical shock.

- Transport to a medical facility.

Radiation Burns

General first aid care for radiation burns is as follows:

- Remove clothing right away, seal it in a suitable container, and label.

- Have the victim shower if possible.

- Whether injuries exist or not, get the victim to an adequate medical facility as soon as possible.

- The facility should be notified in advance that a person exposed to radiation is to be taken there.

Radiation presents a hazard to the rescuer as well as the victim. A rescuer who must enter a radioactive area should stay for as short a time as possible. Radiation is undetectable by the human senses and the rescuer, while attempting to aid the victim, may receive a fatal dose of radiation without realizing it.

Inhalation Injury

Carbon monoxide poisoning and damage to the respiratory tract can cause inhalation problems for the burn victim. The symptoms of carbon monoxide poisoning are headache (an early sympton), dizziness, nausea, unconsciousness or irrational behavior, weak or rapid pulse, shallow respirations or absence of breathing, and dilation of the pupils of the eyes. First aid care for the victim of carbon monoxide poisoning includes artificial ventilation if breathing has stopped, and the administration of 100 percent oxygen if available. Singed nasal hair, swollen nasal membranes, and dried mucous secretions present potential inhalation problems in the upper respiratory system. Damage to the lower portion of the airway may not be obvious for 24 to 48 hours after injury. If inhalation injury is suspected, transport the victim to a medical facility.

Additional Factors That Affect the Chance of Recovery

Children below the age of five and adults over the age of 60 generally have a lower recovery rate than other age groups. Young children and older adults can not withstand the traumatic stress of a severe burn. Alcoholics and drug addicts have high mortality rates even with minor burns. The individual who is overweight also has a lesser chance of survival.

CHAPTER 8. FRACTURES AND DISLOCATIONS

Fractures

A fracture is a broken or cracked bone. Fractures are caused in several ways (figure 8.01):

—Direct blow. The bone is broken at the point of impact. For example, a person is hit in the leg by a piece of flying rock and the bone is broken at the point where the rock hit the leg.

—Indirect blow. The bone is broken by forces traveling along the bone from the point of impact. For example, a person who falls and lands on the hands may suffer a broken arm.

—Twisting forces. A severe twisting force can result in a fracture. For example, a person playing football or skiing is susceptible to this type of injury.

—Muscle contractions. Violent muscle contractions can result in a fracture. For example, a person who receives an electrical shock can experience muscle contractions so as to cause fractures.

—Pathological conditions. Localized disease or aging can weaken bones to the point that the slightest stress may result in a fracture.

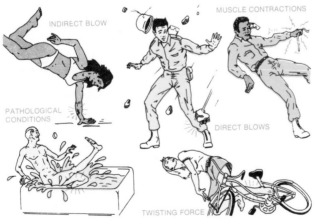

FIGURE 8.01.—Major causes of fractures.

Fractures are typed according to the manner in which the bone is broken. The type of fracture an individual has suffered can be determined only by x-ray. The types of fractures are as follows:

—Transverse fracture. The break is straight across the bone.

—Spiral fracture. The break twists around and through the bone.

—Oblique fracture. The break is at an oblique angle across the bone.

—Comminuted fracture. The bone is fragmented into more than two pieces.

—Impacted fracture. The ends of the broken bones are jammed into each other.

—Greenstick fracture. The break passes only part way through the bone.

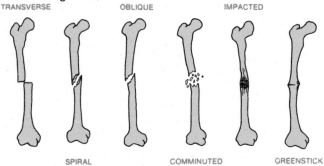

FIGURE 8.02.—Types of fractures.

For first aid purposes fractures can be divided into two classifications (figure 8.03):

—Open (compound) fracture. The bone is broken and an open wound is present. Often the end of the broken bone may protrude from the wound.

—Closed (simple) fracture. The bone is broken, but no open wound is present.

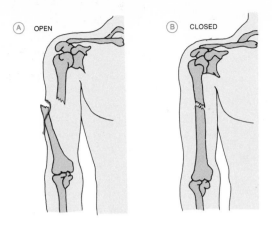

FIGURE 8.03.—Open and closed fractures.

Broken bones, especially the long bones of the upper and lower extremities, often have sharp, sawtooth edges; even slight movement may cause the sharp edges to cut into blood vessels, nerves, or muscles, and perhaps through the skin. Careless or improper handling can convert a simple fracture into a compound fracture, and damage to surrounding blood vessels or nerves can make the injury much more serious. A person handling a fracture should always bear this in mind. Damage due to careless handling of a simple fracture may greatly increase pain and shock, cause complications that will prolong the period of disability, and endanger life through hemorrhage of surrounding blood vessels.

If the broken ends of the bone extend through an open wound, there is little doubt that the victim has suffered fracture. However, the bone does not always extend through the skin, so the person administering first aid care must be able to recognize other signs that the bone may be fractured.

The general signs and symptoms of a fracture are as follows:

—Pain or tenderness in the region of the fracture.

—Deformity or irregularity of the affected area.

—Loss of function (disability) of the affected area.

—Moderate or severe swelling.

—Discoloration.

—Victim's information, if conscious, (the victim may have felt the bone snap or break.)

Be careful when examining injured persons, particularly those apparently suffering fractures. For all fractures the first aider must remember to maintain an open airway, control bleeding, and treat for shock. Do not attempt to change the position of an injured person until the person has been examined and it has been determined that movement will not complicate the injuries. If the victim is lying down, it is far better to attend to the injuries with the victim in that position and with as little movement as possible. If fractures are present, make any necessary movement in such a manner as to protect the injured part against further injury.

Splints

Splints are used to support, immobilize, and protect parts with injuries such as known or suspected fractures, dislocations, or severe sprains. When in doubt, treat the injury as a fracture and splint it. Splints prevent movement at the area of the injury and at the nearest joints. Splints should immobilize and support the joint or bones above and below the break.

Many types of splints are available commercially. Plastic inflatable splints can be easily applied and quickly inflated, require a minimum of dressing and give rigid support to injured limbs (figure 8.04). Improvised splints may be made from pieces of wood, broom handles, heavy cardboard, newspapers, magazines, or similar firm materials.

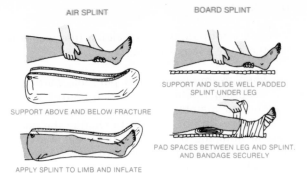

AIR SPLINT

SUPPORT ABOVE AND BELOW FRACTURE

APPLY SPLINT TO LIMB AND INFLATE

BOARD SPLINT

SUPPORT AND SLIDE WELL PADDED
SPLINT UNDER LEG

PAD SPACES BETWEEN LEG AND SPLINT.
AND BANDAGE SECURELY

FIGURE 8.04.—Splinting.

Certain guidelines should be followed when splinting:

- Gently remove all clothing from any suspected fracture or dislocation.

- Do not attempt to push bones back through an open wound.

- Do not attempt to straighten any fracture.

- Cover open wounds with a sterile dressing before splinting.

- Pad splints with soft material to prevent excessive pressure on the affected area and to aid in supporting the injured part.

- Pad under all natural arches of the body such as the knee and wrist.

- Support the injured part while splint is being applied.

- Splint firmly, but not so tightly as to interfere with circulation or cause undue pain.

- Tie all knots on or near the splint.

- Do not transport the victim until the fracture or dislocation has been supported.

- Elevate the injured part and apply ice when possible.

Inflatable splints can be used to immobilize fractures of the lower leg or forearm. When applying inflatable splints (non-zipper type), follow these guidelines:

- Gather splint on your own arm so that the bottom edge is above your wrist.

- Help support the victim's limb or have someone else hold it.

- Take hold of the injured limb, and slide the splint from your forearm over it.

- *Inflate by mouth only* to the desired pressure. The splint should be inflated to the point where your thumb would make a slight indentation.

For a zipper type air splint, lay the victim's limb in the unzipped air splint, zip it and inflate. Traction cannot be maintained when applying this type of splint. Change in temperature can effect air splints, going from a cold area to a warm area will cause the splint to expand. It may be necessary to deflate the splint until proper pressure is reached.

Areas of Fracture

Skull

Any fracture of the skull is considered serious because of the possible injury to the brain. A fracture may occur to any area of the skull. Injuries to the back of the head are particularly dangerous. The skull may be fractured without visible wound to the scalp. The victim of a skull fracture may exhibit the following symptoms:

—Blood or watery fluid may flow from one or both ears, or from the nose and mouth.

—Pupils of the eyes may be dilated or unequal in size. (This would indicate pressure on the brain.)

All serious injuries to the head should be considered possible fractures of the skull, and if doubt exists, treated as such. A person with a skull fracture may also have an injury to the spine.

The first aid care for a skull fracture is as follows:

- Keep the victim quiet and lying down.

- Maintain an open airway.

- If breathing problems occur, place the victim in a three-quarters prone position.

- Place a blanket or other soft material under the head and shoulders.

- Control bleeding from the scalp with minimal pressure and dress the wound; tie the knots of the bandage away from injured area. Do not try to control bleeding from ear or nose.

- Never give a stimulant.

- Keep the victim warm and treat for shock (figure 8.05).

- Keep victim's head from resting on the suspected fracture.

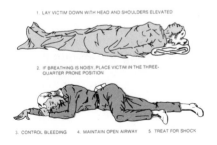

FIGURE 8.05.—First aid for fractured skull.

Nose

A broken nose is a very common type of fracture and may result from any hard blow to the nose. The symptoms of a broken nose are as follows:

—Deformity of the bridge of the nose.

—Pain.

—Bleeding.

—Swelling.

Any blow to the nose that causes bleeding should be treated as a fracture. The first aid care for a broken nose is as follows:

- Apply a bandage compress if there is an open fracture (figure 8.06).

- Take the victim to the doctor.

FIGURE 8.06.—Dressing for an open fracture of the nose.

Upper Jaw

In fractures of the upper jaw or cheekbone, where there is an open wound, treat as for an open wound of the face, but do not tie bandage knots over any wounds (figure 8.07). If there is no open wound, a dressing is not necessary, but the victim should be taken to a doctor.

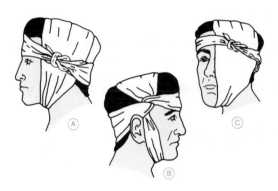

FIGURE 8.07.—Dressing for a fracture of the upper jaw.

Lower Jaw

The symptoms of a fracture of the lower jaw are as follows:

—The mouth is usually open.

—Saliva mixed with blood flows from the mouth.

—The teeth of the lower jaw may be uneven, loosened, or knocked out.

The first aid care for a fracture of the lower jaw is as follows:

• Maintain a clear airway.

- Gently place the jaw in a position so that the lower teeth rest against the upper teeth, if possible.

- Place the center of a cravat bandage over the front of the chin, and pass the ends around the back of the head and tie, leaving the ends long.

- Place the center of a second cravat bandage under the chin, pass the ends over the cheeks to the center of the top of the head, and tie, leaving the ends long.

- Bring the ends of the two bandages together and tie separately (figure 8.08).

- Transport the victim on his or her side to allow drainage.

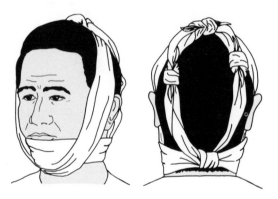

FIGURE 8.08.—Bandage for fracture of lower jaw.

Collarbone

Fracture of the collarbone frequently is caused by a fall with the hand outstretched or by a blow to the shoulder. The symptoms of a fractured collarbone are as follows:

—Pain in the area of the shoulder.

—Partial or total disability of the arm on the injured side.

—The injured shoulder tends to droop.

—The victim frequently supports the injured arm at the elbow or wrist with the other hand.

To support the fracture while transporting the victim proceed as follows:

- Place padding between the arm and the victim's side.

- Put the limb in a sling by placing one end of a cravat bandage over the shoulder on the uninjured side. Carry the other end over the forearm and up the back to the same shoulder and tie.

- Secure the arm to the body with a wide cravat bandage tied over a pad on the opposite side (figure 8.09).

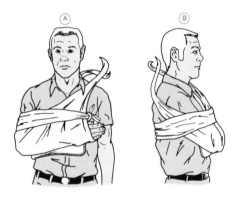

FIGURE 8.09.—Bandage for fracture of collarbone.

Shoulder Blade

Fracture of the shoulder blade is not a common injury. It usually is caused by a direct blow to the shoulder blade and generally results in a closed fracture with little displacement. Symptoms are as follows:

—Pain and swelling at the fracture.

—Inability to swing the arm back and forward from the shoulder.

To support a fracture of the shoulder blade proceed as follows:

- Place the forearm in a triangular sling (A of figure 8.10).

- Bind the arm securely to the chest with a wide cravat bandage extending from the point of the shoulder downward by carrying one end across the chest and the other end across the back.

- Tie over a pad under the opposite armpit.

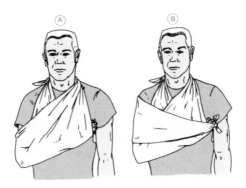

FIGURE 8.10.—Bandage for fracture of shoulder blade.

Upper Portion of the Upper Arm

In order to immobilize a fracture of the upper portion of the upper arm proceed as follows:

- Have an assistant support the fracture on both sides of the break.

- Bind the arm to the rib cage with a wide cravat bandage that is tied over a pad under the opposite armpit (A of figure 8.11).

- Place the forearm in a triangular bandage sling.

The forearm should not be pulled up too high because this will increase pain (B of figure 8.11).

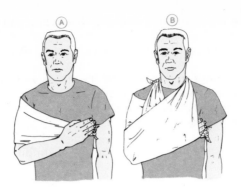

FIGURE 8.11.—Bandage for fracture of upper portion of the upper arm.

Elbow

Extreme care must be taken when dealing with a fractured elbow, as the fracture may cause extensive damage to surrounding tissues, nerves, and blood vessels. Improper care and handling of a fractured elbow could result in a permanent disability. The symptoms of a fracture of the elbow are as follows:

—Extreme pain.

—Extensive discoloration around elbow.

—Swelling.

—Deformity.

—Bone may be visible or projecting from the wound.

The first aid care for a fractured elbow is as follows:

- Do not bend, straighten, or twist the arm in any direction.

- If available, a plastic inflatable splint should be used when the arm is found in a straight position.

- If the arm is bent, immobilize in a bent position (figure 8.12).

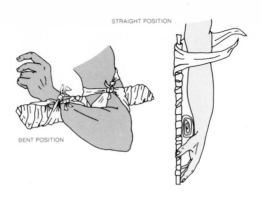

FIGURE 8.12.—Splinting of a fractured elbow.

Forearm and Wrist

Fractures of the forearm and wrist are generally less painful than fractures of the arm, shoulder blade, or elbow. The symptoms of a fractured forearm and wrist are as follows:

—Pain.

—Tenderness.

—Severe deformity, if both bones of the forearm are broken.

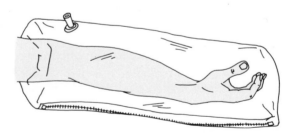

FIGURE 8.13.—Plastic inflatable splint for forearm and wrist.

If available, a plastic inflatable splint should be used to immobilize the forearm or wrist (figure 8.13). If a plastic inflatable
splint is not available, an L-shaped splint for the forearm and
wrist can be made from two pieces of board ¼ inch thick and 4
inches wide. One piece should be long enough to extend from 1
inch below the armpit to the point of the elbow and the other long
enough to extend from the point of the elbow to 1 inch beyond
the end of the middle finger. Immobilize the limb to the splint in
the following manner:

- Fasten the boards together securely to form an L-shaped
  splint.

- Pad the splint.

- While an assistant supports the fracture on both sides of
  the break, apply the splint to the inner side of the arm
  and forearm after the forearm has been bent across the
  chest.

- Use four cravat bandages to hold the splint in place.

- Place the center of the first cravat bandage on the outside
  of the arm at the upper end of the splint, pass around the
  arm one or more times, and tie at the side of the splint.

- Place the centers of the second and third cravats on the
  arm just above and below the elbow and apply in a similar way.

- Apply the fourth cravat bandage by placing the center of
  the bandage on the back of the wrist, passing the ends
  around and crossing on the splint under the wrist; bring
  one end up around the little finger side, passing over the
  back of the hand and down between the forefinger and
  thumb; pass the other end up over the thumb, and cross
  it over the back of the hand down around the little finger
  side; then cross both ends on the splint, and tie on top of
  hand.

- Place the arm in a cravat bandage sling (figure 8.14).

Either splinting procedure may also be used for a fracture of the
lower two-thirds of the arm.

L-SHAPED PADDED
SPLINTS (TWO)

FIGURE 8.14.—Splint for lower two-thirds of arm, forearm, and wrist.

Hand

Fractures of the hand usually result from a direct blow. The symptoms of a fracture of the hand are as follows:

—Acute pain.

—Tenderness.

—Swelling.

—Discoloration.

—Enlarged joints.

If available, a plastic inflatable splint should be used for immobilization. A board splint can be used if a plastic inflatable splint is not available. To immobilize a fractured hand with a board splint, proceed as follows:

- Place padding in the palm of the hand and under the wrist.

- Splint should extend from beyond the fingertips to mid-forearm.

- Secure the hand and forearm to the splint with a roller bandage.

- Place arm in a sling.

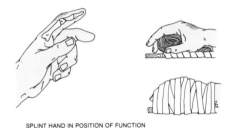

SPLINT HAND IN POSITION OF FUNCTION

FIGURE 8.15.—Bandage for a fracture of the hand or finger.

Rib

Fracture of the rib usually is caused by a direct blow or a severe squeeze. A fracture can occur at any point along the rib. The symptoms of a fractured rib are as follows:

—Severe pain on breathing.

—Tenderness over the fracture.

—Deformity.

—Inability to take a deep breath.

Cravat bandages will immobilize fractured ribs. Place the bandages in the following order:

- Place the arm of the injured side across chest at approximately a 45-degree angle.

- Bind arm to chest with three overlapping medium cravat bandages.

- Tie a fourth bandage along angle of the forearm for support (figure 8.16).

FIGURE 8.16.—Bandage for fracture of the rib.

The chest should not be wrapped when the ribs are depressed and/or frothy blood comes from the victim's mouth. These may be indications of a punctured lung. An open wound from the outside to the lung should be covered immediately with a non pourous material. The victim should be placed in a semi-prone position with the injured side down. This will allow more room for expansion of the uninjured lung.

Spinal Column

The spinal column is composed of 24 bones called vertebra (figure 8.17).

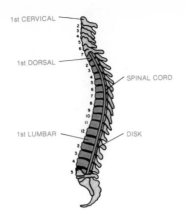

FIGURE 8.17.—Spinal column.

Each vertebra surrounds and protects the spinal cord and specific nerve roots (figure 8.18).

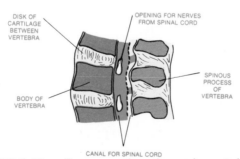

FIGURE 8.18.—Cross section through vertebrae.

Fracture of the spinal column may occur at any point along the backbone between its junction with the head at the top and junction with the pelvic basin below. Where portions of the broken vertebrae are displaced, the spinal cord may be cut, or pressure may be put on the cord (figure 8.19).

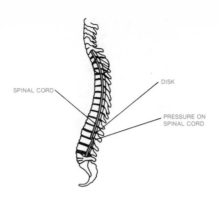

FIGURE 8.19.—Fracture of the spinal column, showing pressure on the spinal cord.

Spinal cord injuries can result in paralysis or death, because they cannot always be corrected by surgery and the spinal cord has very limited self healing powers. For this reason it is extremely important for the person rendering first aid care to be able to recognize the signs of spinal column damage. The following signs and symptoms are associated with spinal injuries:

—Pain and tenderness at the site of the injury.

—Deformity.

—Cuts and bruises.

—Paralysis.

First, check the lower extremities for paralysis. If the victim is conscious, determine the following (figure 8.20):

1. Whether the victim can feel your touch to his feet.

2. Whether the victim can wiggle his/her toes and then to raise his/her legs.

3. Whether the victim can press against your hand with his/her feet.

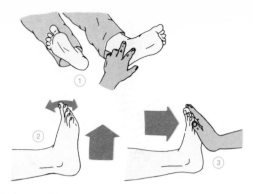

FIGURE 8.20.—Checking for paralysis in the lower extremities when the victim is conscious.

Second, check the upper extremities for paralysis. If the victim is conscious, determine the following (figure 8.21):

1. Whether the victim can feel your touch to his/her hands and arms.

2. Whether the victim can wiggle his/her fingers and then raise his/her arms.

3. Whether the victim can grasp your hand and squeeze.

FIGURE 8.21.—Checking the upper extremities for paralysis when the victim is conscious.

If the victim is unconscious perform the following tests for paralysis (figure 8.22).

1. Stroke the soles of the feet or ankles with a pointed object; if the spinal cord is undamaged, the foot will react.

2. Stroke the palm of the hand with a pointed object; if the spinal cord is undamaged, the hand will react.

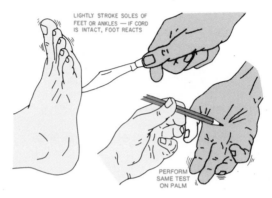

LIGHTLY STROKE SOLES OF FEET OR ANKLES — IF CORD IS INTACT, FOOT REACTS

PERFORM SAME TEST ON PALM

FIGURE 8.22.—Checking for paralysis when the victim is unconscious.

All questionable injuries to the spinal column, even in the absence of signs of paralysis should be treated as a fracture of the spinal column. The initial care that the victim receives at the scene of the accident is extremely important. Proper care, not speed, is essential. Improper care or handling could result in paralysis or death. The first aid care for an individual with a fractured spinal column is as follows:

• Apply traction to the head, immobilizing it in line with the rest of the body (figure 8.23). Tension should be on the long axis of the spine. Pull from the lower edges of jaw without tilting head. Do not release traction until victim is secured to a splint, stretcher, or other hard, flat surface which provides firm support (see chapter 9).

• Use a blanket, padding, or a cervical collar around the head and neck.

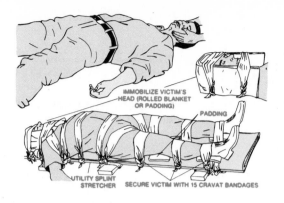

FIGURE 8.23.—Immobilization of head and neck.

- Maintain an open airway.

- Control bleeding and dress any wounds.

- Use enough people to safely lift the victim as a unit and place the victim on his or her back on the splint or stretcher (see chapter 9).

- The victim should only be lifted high enough to slide the splint or stretcher underneath.

- Secure the victim to the splint or stretcher so that the entire body is immobilized.

- Cover with a blanket and treat for shock.

- Transport the victim on his or her back.

Pelvis or Hip

Fracture of the pelvis or hip usually results from a squeeze through the hips or a direct blow. Extreme care is needed when handling an individual with a fracture of the pelvis or hip because there is a strong possibility of associated internal injuries to the digestive, urinary, or genital organs. The symptoms of a fractured pelvis or hip are as follows:

—Pain is felt in the pelvic region.

—Discoloration is present.

—The victim is unable to raise his or her leg.

—The affected leg is usually turned outward.

To support the pelvic region before the victim is transported proceed as follows:

- Maintain support of the pelvic region with hands at the sides of the hips until the bandages have been applied.

- Place the center of a wide cravat bandage over one hip, the upper edge extending about 2 inches above the crest of the hip bone.

- Pass the ends around the body and tie over a pad on the opposite hip.

- Place the center of a second wide cravat bandage over the opposite hip, the upper edge extending about 2 inches above the crest of the hipbone.

- Pass the ends around the body and tie over a pad on the first bandage.

- Lift the victim high enough to place him on a *firm* support, either a basket stretcher, utility splint, or stretcher board (see chapter 9).

- Secure the victim to the stretcher, utility splint, or stretcher board (figure 8.24).

- Cover the victim with a blanket and treat for shock.

- Get the victim to the doctor or hospital.

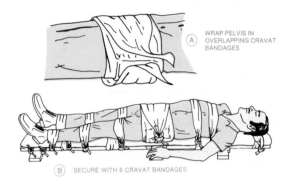

FIGURE 8.24.—Immobilization of fracture of pelvis.

Thigh or Knee

If a fracture of the thigh or knee is open, the wound should be dressed. If the fracture is at the knee joint and the limb is not in a straight position, make no attempt to straighten the limb. Attempts to straighten the limb may increase the possibility of permanent damage. Improvise a way to immobilize the knee as it is found, using padding to fill any space. The utility splint stretcher or a similar support (see chapter 9) may be used to immobilize fractures of the knee or thigh. Before the victim is placed on the stretcher, it should be well padded and tested. Additional padding will also be necessary for the natural arches of the body. The victim must be carefully raised for placement on the stretcher while the fracture is supported from the underside on both sides of the break.

Apply the splint with bandages. All bandages should be tied on the injured side near the splint.

- Tie the first bandage around the body and splint under the armpits.

- Tie the second around the chest and splint and the third around the hips and splint.

- Tie the fourth and fifth bandages just below the knee and at the ankle of the injured leg.

- Tie sixth and seventh bandages at the thigh and ankle of the uninjured leg (figure 8.25).

- The victim should be transported on a regular stretcher or stretcher board.

FIGURE 8.25.—Splint for fracture of the thigh.

If a stretcher board (see chapter 9) is used, it should be well padded and the bandages applied in normal order. On some types of stretcher boards it may be necessary to tie both lower limbs together with each of the last four cravat bandages. To prevent movement of the legs, pad well between the legs before applying the cravats.

Any improvised splint for the thigh or knee should be long enough to immobilize the hip and the ankle.

Knee or Kneecap

A splint suitable for a broken back may also be used for fractures of the knee or kneecap. Dress any open wound first. The splint should be will padded with additional padding under all natural body arches. Support the fractures from the top and on both sides and carefully raise the victim to place the prepared and tested splint underneath.

Apply the splint with seven cravat bandages. Tie all bandages on the injured side near the splint.

- Tie three bandages around the body and the splint; one just below the armpits, and around the chest, and one around the hips.

- Tie the fourth bandage around the thigh and splint just below the crotch.

- Place the center of the fifth bandage just above the kneecap and bring the ends under the thigh and splint but do not tie.

- Place the center of the sixth bandage just below the kneecap, bring the ends under the thigh and splint but do not tie.

- Place the center of the sixth bandage just below the kneecap, bring the ends under the leg and splint up over the thigh and tie above the knee over the fifth bandage.

- Pull the ends of the fifth bandage tight and tie below the knee over the sixth bandage.

- The last bandage is tied around the ankle and splint (figure 8.26).

The victim should be transported on a regular stretcher.

FIGURE 8.26.—Splint for fracture of knee or kneecap.

Any stretcher board used for this type of injury should be the type of board which is prepared for individual bandaging of each lower extremity. Otherwise, the bandages would necessarily be applied as for fracture of thigh or knee.

Any improvised splint for the kneecap should be long enough to immobilize the hip and the ankle.

Leg or Ankle

If the fracture is open, dress the wound before splinting. When it is necessary to remove a shoe or boot because of severe pain from swelling of the ankle or for any other reason, the removal must be carefully done by unlacing or cutting the boot to prevent damage to the ankle. In the absence of severe swelling or bleeding it may be wise to leave the boot on for additional support.

The splint for a fracture of the leg or ankle should reach from against the buttocks to beyond the heel. It should be well padded and placed under the victim while the leg is supported on both sides of the fracture. Tie the bandages on the outer side, near the splint.

With a cravat bandage make one wrap of the upper end of the splint and padding before the splint is placed under the victim. When the splint is in place, bandage as follows:

- Pass the end of this first bandage around the inner side of the thigh, high in the groin, pass it over the thigh, under the splint, and tie.

- Pass two bandages around the thigh and splint, one at the middle of the thigh and the other just above the knee. Tie.

- Place additional padding around the knee and ankle.

- Place a padded splint on the outer side of the leg (figure 8.27).

- Pass a fourth bandage around the leg, the padding, and the splint just below the knee and tie; pass a fifth just above or below the fracture and tie.

- Pass the center of a sixth bandage around the instep and over the additional padding and bring the ends up each side of the ankle.

- Cross the ends on top and pass them around the ankle, padding, and splint.

- Cross the ends under the splint, return to the top of the ankle, cross and carry down each side of the ankle and tie under the instep.

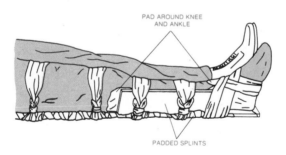

PAD AROUND KNEE AND ANKLE

PADDED SPLINTS

FIGURE 8.27.—Splint for fracture of leg or ankle.

If an inflatable plastic splint is used, roll up or cut away the clothing from the limb to a point above the upper end of the splint. The splint should be long enough to immobilize the knee as well as the ankle (figure 8.28). Open wounds should be covered with gauze, but they need not be bandaged because the splint will form an airtight cover for such wounds. Pressure from the inflated splint will control any bleeding that may develop after the splint is applied, but it is recommended that a loose tourniquet be applied above the area the splint will cover, in case bleeding develops while the splint is being applied. Apply the splint while supporting the fracture on both sides. Close and inflate the splint.

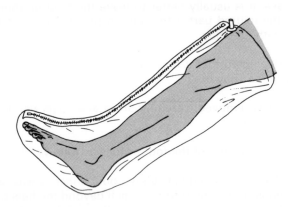

FIGURE 8.28.—Inflatable plastic splint for fracture of leg or ankle.

Improvised splints for the leg should be long enough to immobilize the knee and ankle. An improvised splint for the ankle may be made from a blanket or pillow by carefully folding it around the ankle and foot and securing with several bandages. Padding should then be placed between the legs and the legs tied together (figure 8.29).

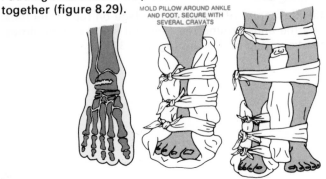

FIGURE 8.29.—Immobilization of ankle or foot.

Foot or Toes

When caring for a fracture of the foot or toes, a boot or shoe should be left in place if possible and supported. If it is necessary to remove any type of footwear, extreme care must be taken. If the protective cap of a safety boot has been damaged in such a way as to become embedded in the foot, do not remove the boot. In any case, it is usually better to leave the boot or shoe on and support the injured part if the injured person can be taken to a hospital without delay.

It should be noted that it may be impossible to use an inflatable splint with the shoe on.

If footwear is removed, carefully dress any open wounds before applying a splint.

Immobilize a fracture of the foot or toes as follows:

- Place a well padded splint, about 4 inches wide and long enough to extend from ½ inch beyond the heel to ½ inch beyond the big toe, on the bottom of the foot.

- Start the center of a cravat bandage around the ankle from the back just above the heel; cross over the arch and carry under the foot and splint; cross under the splint and bring the ends to the back of the heel; cross the back of the heel, carry the ends around the ankle and tie in front.

- Start the center of a second bandage on top of the toes, carry the ends around the foot and splint several times, then tie on top of the foot (figure 8.30).

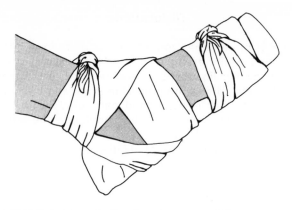

FIGURE 8.30.—Splint for fracture of foot or toes.

An air splint specifically made for the foot and ankle may be used
(figure 8.31) or an improvised splint made from a blanket or pillow as in caring for a fractured ankle (figure 8.29).

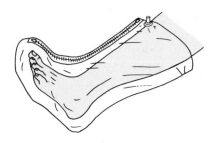

FIGURE 8.31.—Inflatable plastic splint for fracture of foot.

Dislocations

Where two or more bones come together, they form a joint. The bones forming a joint are held in place by bands of strong, fibrous tissue known as ligaments. There are three varieties of joints: immovable joints, joints with limited motion, and freely movable joints. The first aider is concerned particularly with the freely movable joints—the lower jaw, the shoulders, the elbows, the wrists, the fingers, the hips, the knees, the ankles, and the toes. These are the joints most commonly dislocated.

A dislocation is the slipping out of normal position of one or more of the bones forming a joint. The ligaments holding the bones in proper position are stretched and sometimes torn loose. Fractures are often associated with dislocations.

Dislocations may result from the following:

      —Force applied at or near the joint.

      —Sudden muscular contractions.

      —Twisting strains on joint ligaments.

      —Falls where the force of landing is transferred to a joint.

Some general symptoms of dislocation are as follows:

      —Rigidity and loss of function.

      —Deformity.

      —Pain.

      —Swelling.

      —Tenderness.

      —Discoloration.

General First Aid Care for Dislocations

Reducing dislocations requires skill in manipulating the parts so as not to damage further the joint ligaments and the numerous blood vessels and nerves found close to joints. Only a physician should reduce dislocations. Because of the pain involved, one exception may be a dislocated jaw. Where medical aid is readily available, do not attempt reduction of even this dislocation.

Care for dislocations by applying splints and/or dressings to immobilize the joint in the line of deformity in which it is found, and obtain medical treatment.

Areas of Dislocation

Lower Jaw

The symptoms of a dislocated lower jaw are as follows:

—Pain.

—Open mouth.

—Rigid jaw.

—Difficulty in speaking.

If medical aid is not available for some time, reduce the dislocation as follows:

- Wrap both your thumbs in several layers of clean cloth.

- Stand behind victim with the victim's head resting against your stomach.

- Place the wrapped thumbs in the victim's mouth, resting them well back on each side of the lower teeth.

- Seize the outside of the lower jaw with the fingers.

- Press first downward and forward.

- When the jaw starts into place, slip the thumbs off the teeth to the inside of the cheeks.

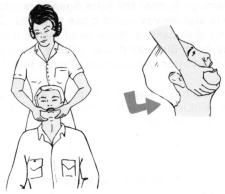

FIGURE 8.32.—Reducing a dislocated jaw.

- Place the center of a cravat bandage over the front of the chin.

- Carry the ends to the back of the head and tie.

- Center another bandage under the victim's chin, bring the ends to the tip of the head and tie (A of figure 8.33).

- Bring the ends of both bandages together and tie them separately (B of figure 8.33). If difficulty is experienced in reducing a dislocated lower jaw, do not make repeated attempts to reduce the dislocation. Apply no dressing, but have the victim taken to a doctor immediately.

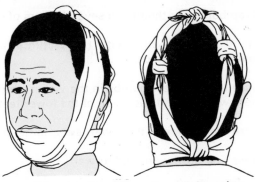

FIGURE 8.33.—Dressing for lower jaw dislocation.

Shoulder

The shoulder joint usually is dislocated by falls or blows directly on the shoulder or by falls on the hand or elbow. The symptoms of a dislocated shoulder are as follows:

—The elbow stands off 1 or 2 inches from the body.

—The arm is held rigid.

—The shoulder appears flat.

—A marked depression is evident beneath the point of the shoulder.

—Pain and swelling are present at the site of the injury.

—The victim cannot bring the elbow in contact with the side. While the arm is being supported in the position in

While the arm is being supported in the position in which it was found, immobilize the shoulder in the following manner:

- Place the point of a wedge-shaped pad (4 inches wide and 1 to 3 inches thick) between the arm and the body.

- Tape or tie the pad in place.

- Place the center of a medium width cravat on the outside of the arm just above the elbow.

- Carry one end across the chest, the other end across the back.

- Tie on the opposite side of the chest over a pad (figure 8.34).

- Place the arm in a triangular bandage sling.

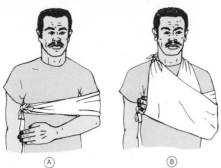

FIGURE 8.34.—Dressing for dislocation of shoulder.

Elbow

Dislocation occurs at the elbow joint as a result of a blow at the joint or occasionally by a fall on the hand. It usually can be recognized by these symptoms:

—Deformity at the joint.

—Inability to bend the limb at the joint.

—Great pain.

The elbow must be immobilized in the line of deformity in which it was found. While the elbow is being supported, proceed as follows:

- Prepare and pad a splint—straight, L-shaped, or a modification of the latter depending on the position of the limb.

- Secure the splint on the inside of the limb.

- Bind the limb to the body or place the forearm in a cravat bandage sling.

In some instances, the entire limb may be tied to the body or other means of immobilizing may be found when regular splinting material is not available.

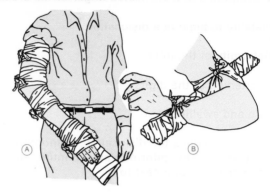

FIGURE 8.35.—Immobilization of elbow.

Wrist

Dislocation of the wrist usually occurs when the hand is extended to break the force of a fall. It is difficult, however, to distinguish between a dislocation and a fractured wrist. Treat a suspected dislocated wrist the same as a fractured one (figure 8.36).

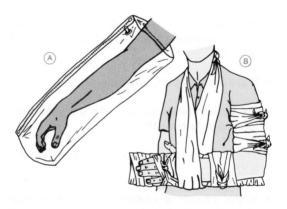

FIGURE 8.36.—Splint for dislocation of wrist.

Finger or Toe

The usual symptoms of a dislocated finger or toe areas follows:

—Inability to bend at a dislocation.

—Deformity of the joint.

—Shortening of the digit.

—Pain and swelling.

Do not attempt to reduce the dislocation. Immobilize the digit by using small pads for any deformity and splinting, or by tying the injured member to the one next to it.

Hip

Dislocation of the hip usually results from falling onto the foot or knee. It may also be caused by a direct blow when the thigh is at the angle with the spine.

While supporting the dislocation in the line of deformity, carefully raise the victim only high enough to be placed on a well-padded and tested splint or stretcher board suitable for a broken back (see chapter 9). Support is necessary until the splint or stretcher board is applied.

- Make a tapered pad of clothing, blankets, or other material large enough to support the limb in the line of deformity.

- Place a small pad between the feet.

- Tie all bandages around the body and the splint on the injured side near the splint.

- The last bandage should tie the feet together (figure 8.37).

- If the victim is unconscious, the forearm should be placed in a basket sling.

157

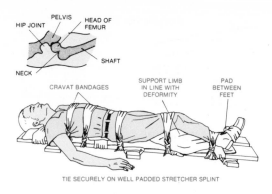

FIGURE 8.37.—Splint for dislocation of hip.

If a splint or stretcher board has been tested, it may be used as a stretcher for transportation. However, when the broken-back splint is used, it is better to place and tie it on a regular stretcher, properly tested, for transportation.

Knee or Kneecap

Dislocation of the knee or kneecap results from direct force applied at the knee or from a fall on the knee. The symptoms of the dislocation are as follows:

—Deformity.

—Inability to use the knee.

—Great pain.

While supporting the dislocation, apply a splint as for fracture of the thigh, using either a broken-back splint or a stretcher board. Place extra padding of blankets, clothes, or similar material to conform to any deformity.

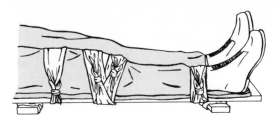

FIGURE 8.38.—Splint for dislocation of knee or kneecap.

Ankle

Dislocation of the ankle may show several types of deformity. Bones are almost always broken. There is a marked deformity at the joint. As a rule, swelling is rapid and marked and great pain is felt.

While supporting the dislocation, apply a splint as for a fracture of the leg or ankle, and add padding to conform to the deformity (A of figure 8.39). An air splint long enough to immobilize the knee may be used or a blanket or pillow may be used to splint (B of figure 8.39).

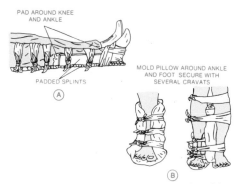

FIGURE 8.39.—Immobilization of ankle.

CHAPTER 9. HANDLING AND TRANSPORTATION OF AN INJURED PERSON

After receiving first aid care, an injured person often requires transportation to a medical facility. It is the responsibility of the first aider to see that the victim is transported in such a manner as to prevent further injury and is not subjected to unnecessary pain or discomfort. Improper handling and careless transportation often add to the original injuries, increase shock, and endanger life.

Under normal circumstances a victim should not be moved until a thorough examination has been made and first aid care has been rendered. A seriously injured person should be moved in a position that is least likely to aggravate injuries. Various methods for carrying a victim can be used in emergencies, but the stretcher is the preferred method of transportation. When a stretcher is unavailable or impractical, other means of transportation may be employed.

Two-Person Seat Carry

The two-person seat carry is a technique for transporting the victim in a seat fashioned from the rescuers' arms (figure 9.01). It provides for speedy removal and can be used when the victim must be moved through narrow passageways. This carry should not be used when there is indication of damage to the spinal column.

FIGURE 9.01.—Two-person seat carry.

Three-Person Carry

The three-person lift and carry may be used when an injured person is to be carried a short distance or transported through narrow passageways, or when a stretcher is not available. The lift is also used when an injured person is being placed on or removed from a stretcher.

Three persons are required for this lift, and a fourth is desirable. Lifting must be done on command of one person.

To perform the three-person lift and carry, proceed as follows:

- Each of the three rescuers kneels on the knee nearest the victim's feet and on the least injured side, if possible.

- One bearer, opposite the victim's shoulders, supports the victim's neck and shoulders (A of figure 9.02).

- One bearer, opposite the victim's hips, supports victim's thighs and small of back.

- The other bearer, opposite the victim's knees, supports the victim's knees and ankles.

- On command, the bearers slowly raise the victim in a prone position to rest on their knees (B of figure 9.02).

- On command, the bearers slowly roll the victim on his or her side so that the victim rests in the bend of their elbows and is held closely to their chests.

- When the command is given, all bearers rise in unison (C of figure 9.02).

- The bearers can then, when commanded, step off in any direction.

FIGURE 9.02.—Three-Person lift and carry.

Stretchers

Canvas Stretcher

The canvas-type stretcher consists of canvas stretched between two poles. The poles are long enough to afford handholds for the bearers at each end (figure 9.03).

FIGURE 9.03.—Canvas-type stretcher.

Basket Stretcher

Various types of basket stretchers are also used to transport the injured. After the victim has been secured by means of straps and foot braces, the basket may be transported even in a vertical position (figure 9.04).

FIGURE 9.04.—Basket stretcher.

Spine Boards

The long spine board is made of high-grade marine plywood. It acts as a splint for the entire body and the victim is secured by straps.

The short spine board is similar in construction but supports only the back and neck. It is used in removing a victim from a vehicle (figure 9.05).

FIGURE 9.05.—Spine boards.

Scoop Stretcher

The scoop stretcher is another means for lifting and transporting a victim. A minimum of body movement in placing the victim on the stretcher is its prime advantage. Both sides of the victim must be accessible to utilize this type of stretcher. The frame halves are slid under the victim from either side. Pinching the victim or catching the clothing between the stretcher halves is prevented by lifting the victim by the clothes as the stretcher is being closed (figure 9.06).

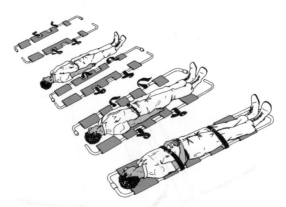

FIGURE 9.06.—Scoop stretcher.

Stretcher Board

A stretcher board is made from a wide board approximately 1½ inches thick, or from laminated plywood about ¾ inch thick. The length is usually about 78 inches and the width 18 inches. Slots about 1 inch wide are placed along the edges. Cravat bandages are passed through these slots to secure the victim to the board. The slots also serve as hand-holds. Some variations have additional slots in the center of the boards so that each leg may be secured separately to the board.

Improvised Stretchers

A satisfactory stretcher may be improvised with a blanket, canvas, brattice cloth, or a strong sheet, and two poles or pieces of pipe, 7 to 8 feet long. To construct an improvised stretcher using two poles and a blanket, proceed as follows:

- Place one pole about 1 foot from the center of the unfolded blanket.

- Fold the short side of the blanket over the pole.

- Place the second pole on the two thicknesses of the blanket about 2 feet from the first pole and parallel to it.

- Fold the remaining side of the blanket over the second pole (figure 9.07). When the victim is placed on the blanket, the weight of the body secures the folds.

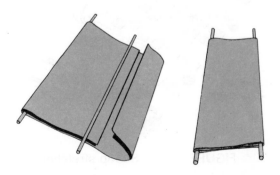

FIGURE 9.07.—Improvised stretcher.

Cloth bags or sacks may be used for stretcher beds. Holes should be made in the bottoms of bags or sacks, so that the poles may be passed through them. Enough bags or sacks should be used to give the length of the bed required. A stretcher may also be made from three or four coats or jackets. The sleeves should be turned inside out with the jacket fastened and the sleeves inside the coat. A pole should be placed through each sleeve.

Utility Splint Stretcher

The utility splint stretcher is a permanently assembled wooden stretcher with pipe runners to add strength and provide hand-holds. It is constructed from two 78-inch 1-by-6 boards and three 21-inch 2-by-4 boards. The 2-by-4's are used as crosspieces. Pipe runners are constructed of ¾ inch pipe that is long enough to extend well past the ends of the long boards. To construct a utility splint stretcher, proceed as follows:

- One crosspiece is permanently fastened 15 inches from one end of the long boards.

- Another crosspiece is permanently fastened 2 inches from the other end of the long boards.

- The remaining crosspiece is not attached to the long boards; it is instead attached to the pipe runners in such a manner as to permit adjustment to any position along the length of the boards.

- If the pipe is not used, the crosspiece is attached to the boards.

- The pipe runners are permanently attached to the crosspieces at the head and foot.

- The center crosspiece is attached to the pipe runners in such a manner as to permit adjustment to any position along the stretcher (figure 9.08).

A splint stretcher can be used for a dislocated hip, dislocated knee, fractured neck, fractured back, fractured pelvis, and all fractures of the lower extremities.

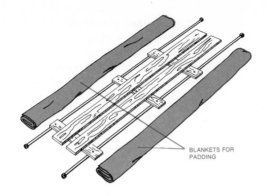

BLANKETS FOR
PADDING

FIGURE 9.08.—Utility splint stretcher.

Stretcher Transportation

When the canvas stretcher is to be used to transport a victim, care should be taken to see that the crosspieces are locked in place (figure 9.09).

Any stretcher should be tested to determine servicability immediately prior to placing an injured person on it. This should be done by placing an uninjured person weighing as much or more than the victim face down on the stretcher. The stretcher is then lifted waist high and lowered to the ground (figure 9.10). Once the stretcher has been tested, it should be padded with a blanket or similar material.

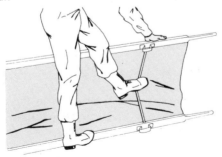

FIGURE 9.09.—Opening the stretcher.

FIGURE 9.10.—Testing the stretcher.

When lifting a victim for stretcher transportation it is preferable to have four or more persons to lift. If only four persons are available and a spinal injury is not suspected, the following method is recommended:

- Each of the four bearers rests on the knee nearest the victim's feet. Three of the bearers position themselves on the victim's least injured side, at the victim's knees, at the hips, and at the shoulders. The fourth bearer is positioned at the victim's hips on the opposite side from the others.

- The hands of the bearer at the shoulders are placed under the victim's neck and shoulders.

- The hands of the bearer at the knees are placed under the victim's knees and ankles.

- The other two bearers each place their hands under the victim's pelvis and the small of the back.

- The four bearers slowly lift the victim, keeping the body level.

- The victim is rested on the knees of the three bearers on the same side.

- The fourth bearer places the stretcher under the victim.

- The bearer who has placed the stretcher assumes his or her original position.

- The victim is gently lowered to the stretcher and covered with a blanket.

- The bearers position themselves one at each end and one at each side of the stretcher, facing the victim.

- All bearers grasp and lift the stretcher.

- The two bearers in the center shift one hand toward the victim's feet and support this end, while the bearer at the victim's feet turns around to a marching position.

- The victim is usually transported feet first so that the bearer at the victim's head can constantly monitor the victim's condition.

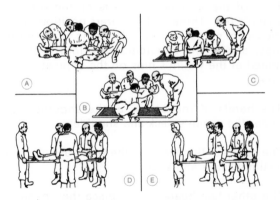

FIGURE 9.11.—Stretcher transportation.

CHAPTER 10. MEDICAL EMERGENCIES

Heat Stroke (Sun Stroke)

Heat stroke is a sudden attack of illness from exposure to the direct rays of the sun or from high temperature without exposure to the sun. Physical exertion is definitely a contributing factor, and heat stroke is more likely to occur in high humidity than in low.

The most important characteristic of heat stroke is the high body temperature which is caused by a disturbance in the heat-regulating mechanism. The person can no longer sweat, and this causes a rise in body temperature.

This illness is more common in persons over age 40. Males are more vulnerable to heat stroke than females. Alcoholics are very susceptible to heat stroke.

The signs and symptoms of heat stroke are as follows:

—The skin is flushed, very hot and very dry.

—Perspiration is absent.

—The pulse is strong and rapid.

—The body temperature can reach 106 to 112 degrees.

—The victim rapidly becomes unconscious.

Care should be centered around lowering the body temperature as quickly as possible. Failure to do this may result in permanent brain damage or death.

The first-aid care for heat stroke is as follows:

• Maintain an open airway.

• Move the victim to a cool environment.

• Remove as much clothing as possible.

- Use cold applications on the head and body.

- Immerse in a cool bath if possible.

- Wrap in a cool sheet; use a fan if available.

- Get the victim to medical help as quickly as possible.

- Watch the individual for relapse and repeated elevated temperatures.

Heat Exhaustion

Heat exhaustion occurs in individuals working in hot environments. It is brought about by the pooling of blood in the vessels under the skin. The blood brings the heat from the interior of the body to the surface in an attempt to cool the body. This increase in blood flow to the surface causes a decrease in the amount of circulating blood and may lead to an inadequate return to the heart and brain and eventually to physical collapse.

This illness occurs most commonly to persons not accustomed to hot weather, those who are overweight, and those who perspire excessively. Women are generally more susceptible to heat exhaustion than men. The signs and symptoms of heat exhaustion are as follows (figure 10.01):

—Pale and clammy skin.

—Profuse perspiration.

—Rapid and shallow breathing.

—Weakness.

—Dizziness.

—Headache.

—In some cases, faintness.

The first aid care for heat exhaustion is as follows:

- Move the victim to as cool and comfortable a place as possible, but do not allow chilling.

- Loosen the victim's clothing.

- If fainting seems likely, have the victim lie down with feet elevated 8 to 12 inches.

- If the victim is conscious, give sips of cool salt water (1 teaspoonful of salt per quart of water). Sugar should be added if possible.

- Treat the victim the same as for shock.

Heat Cramps

Heat cramps affect people who work in a hot environment and perspire. The perspiration causes a loss of salt from the body and if there is inadequate replacement, the body will then suffer from cramps. Heat cramps may also result from drinking iced water or other cold drinks in too large quantities or too quickly.

Signs and symptoms of heat cramps are as follows:

—Muscle cramps or spasms in the leg or abdomen which may be painful.

—Faintness.

—Profuse perspiration.

First-aid care for heat cramps is as follows:

- Move the victim to a cool environment.

- If the victim is conscious, give sips of cool salt and sugar water (1 teaspoon of salt plus as much sugar as the person can stand, per quart of water).

- Massage the cramped areas.

FIGURE 10.01.—Heat exhaustion.

Frostbite

Frostbite results from exposure to severe cold. It is more likely to occur when the wind is blowing, taking heat from the body rapidly. The nose, cheeks, ears, toes, and fingers are the body parts most frequently frostbitten. As a result of exposure to cold, the blood vessels constrict. Thus the blood supply to the chilled parts decreases and the tissues do not get the warmth they need.

The signs and symptoms of frostbite are not always apparent to the victim. Since frostbite has a numbing effect, the victim may not be aware of it until told by someone.

Frostbite goes through the following stages:

—First the skin becomes red.

—As exposure continues, the skin becomes gray or blotchy white.

—The exposed surface becomes numb due to reduced circulation.

—If frostbite or freezing is allowed to continue, all sensation is lost and the skin becomes a "dead" white.

First aid care for frostbite is as follows:

- Wrap and keep the victim as warm and dry as possible until brought indoors.

- Lower the affected part to increase circulation.

- Place gauze pads between fingers and toes if affected.

- Bring the victim indoors.

- Place frostbitten extremities in warm water (102 to 105 F) and make sure the water remains warm. Test the warmth of the water by pouring some on the inner surface of the forearm.

- Apply warm cloths to areas that cannot be submerged.

- Allow the victim to drink hot, stimulating fluids such as coffee or tea.

- Never thaw frostbitten areas if the person will have to go outdoors into the cold again, as this will refreeze thawed areas.

- Do not rub, chafe, or manipulate frostbitten parts.

- Do not use hot water bottles or heat lamps.

- Do not place the victim near a stove or fire, because excessive heat can cause further tissue damage.

- Discourage the victim from smoking, because tobacco constricts the blood vessels.

- Do not allow the victim to walk if the feet are frostbitten.

- Once thawed, have the victim gently exercise the frostbitten areas to stimulate the return of circulation.

- For serious frostbite, seek medical aid for thawing because the pain will be intense and tissue damage extensive.

Hypothermia

Hypothermia is a general cooling of the entire body. The inner core of the body is chilled so the body cannot generate heat to stay warm. This condition can be produced by exposure to low temperatures or to temperatures between 30 and 50 F with wind and rain. Also contributing to hypothermia are fatigue, hunger, and poor physical condition.

Exposure begins when the body loses heat faster that it can be produced. When the body is chilled, it passes through several stages:

    —The initial response of a person exposed to cold is to voluntarily exercise in order to stay warm.

    —As the body tissue is cooled, the person begins to shiver as a result of an involuntary adjustment by the body to preserve normal temperature in the vital organs. Up to this point the person can foresee and take steps to prevent hypothermia. However, these responses drain the body's energy reserves.

If exposure continues until the victim's energy reserves are exhausted, the following symptoms appear:

    —Cold reaches the brain and deprives the victim of judgment and reasoning powers.

    —The victim experiences feelings of apathy, listlessness, and indifference.

    —The victim does not realize what is happening.

    —The victim loses control of the hands.

Cooling becomes more rapid as the internal body temperature is lowered. Eventually hypothermia will result in stupor, collapse, and even death.

The victim of hypothermia may not recognize the symptoms and deny that medical attention is needed. Therefore, it is important to judge the symptoms rather than what the victim says. Even mild symptoms of hypothermia need immediate medical care.

First aid care for a victim of hypothermia is as follows:

- Get the victim out of the elements (wind, rain, snow, cold, etc.)

- Remove all wet clothing.

- Get the victim into dry clothing or wrap the victim in warm blankets.

- Provide external heat by any possible means such as hot water bottles or even body heat from rescuers. Be careful that any external source of heat does not burn the victim.

- If the victim is conscious, give something warm to drink. (Never give alcoholic beverages.)

- If the victim is conscious, try to keep the victim awake.

Diabetic Emergencies

Body and brain cells need many different types of nourishment, one of which is sugar. The circulatory system carries sugar and transfers it to the cells with the aid of a chemical substance called insulin. The pancreas, located in the abdominal cavity, manufactures insulin. When the insulin production and sugar are in balance, the body functions normally. An individual suffering from an imbalance in the production of insulin is said to have diabetes. As a result of this imbalance, the body is adversely affected. However, a great many diabetics lead healthy, normal lives through a program of a balanced diet and medication. When the diabetic's condition is not controlled, certain disorders may occur. The major adverse reactions to insulin imbalance are diabetic coma and insulin shock.

Diabetic Coma

Diabetic coma is a result of an inadequate insulin supply. This imbalance is generally due to a diabetic not taking the proper medication; a diabetic ingesting more sugar than the insulin can accommodate; a person contracting an infection which affects insulin production; or a person vomiting or sustaining fluid loss.

The signs and symptoms of a diabetic coma are as follows:

—Red and dry skin.

—Flushed face.

—Rapid and labored breathing.

—Sickly sweet odor of acetone (similar to nail polish remover or spoiled fruit) on the breath.

—A state of confusion, disorientation, and stupor similar to drunkenness.

The first aid care for the victim of a diabetic coma is as follows:

• Treat the victim the same as for physical shock.

• Place the victim in a semi-reclining position.

• In case of vomiting, turn the head to one side.

• Transport the victim to a medical facility as quickly as possible.

Insulin Shock

Insulin shock results when there is a shortage of sugar relative to the amount of insulin in the body. The prime reasons for the condition are that the person has not eaten, so that not enough sugar has been taken in; the person has taken too much insulin; or the person has over exercised, thus burning sugar too fast.

The signs and symptoms of insulin shock are as follows:

—Personality change in the early stages.

—Profuse perspiration.

—Respiration normal or shallow.

—Rapid, weak pulse.

—Dizziness.

—Cold, clammy skin.

—Convulsions or total unconsciousness.

The first aid care for insulin shock is as follows:

- If the victim is conscious, sugar can be administered in the form of orange juice, a candy bar, soft drinks, or several packets of sugar mixed with orange juice.

- If the victim is unconscious, place granulated sugar under the tongue as rapidly as it dissolves. It is then absorbed into the blood stream.

- Don't worry about the amount of sugar given to the victim, as the doctor will balance the need for sugar against insulin production when the victim arrives at the hospital.

- The victim should be transported to a medical facility for continuing care as quickly as possible.

Epileptic Seizure

Epilepsy is a neurological disorder, usually of unknown origin. Grand mal and petit mal are the two most common types of epilepsy. Of these two, grand mal is more severe.

The signs and symptoms of a grand mal seizure are as follows:

—The victim may have a premonition or aura before the attack occurs.

—Convulsions or loss of consciousness occur.

—Severe spasms of the jaw muscles sometimes occur, causing the tongue to be bitten.

—The face is usually pale before the seizure and becomes cyanotic (bluish) during the seizure.

—Breathing may be loud and labored with a peculiar hissing sound.

—The victim froths at the mouth.

—The seizure only lasts for a few minutes, but it may be followed by another attack.

The petit mal attack is characterized by the following:

—Only a partial loss of consciousness, if any, occurs.

—The victim remains aware of what is going on nearby.

—The victim may experience minor convulsive movements of the eyes or extremities.

The following first aid care for epileptic seizure should be given as necessary:

- The victim should be kept calm.

- Do not restrain the victim.

- Protect the victim from injury by moving objects that could cause harm.

- Place padding under the victim's head.

- Place a padded object between the victim's jaws to prevent biting the tongue. Do this only if the seizure is not in progress as the rescuer can cause equal damage by forcibly attempting to insert an object. A shirt tail and stick can be used for the padded object. Fingers should never be placed in the victim's mouth.

- Do not force the jaws open if they are already clamped shut.

When the seizure is over, do the following:

- Maintain an open airway.

- Allow the victim to rest.

- Protect the victim from stress or embarrassment.

Stroke

A stroke occurs when the blood supply carrying oxygen to the brain is cut off due to a blockage or rupture of a blood vessel. The effects of a stroke on the brain can be temporary or permanent, and range from slight to severe.

—Cerebral thrombosis is a blockage of the cerebral artery by a clot which, forms inside the artery.

—Cerebral hemorrhage occurs when a diseased artery in the brain ruptures and floods the surrounding tissue with blood.

—Cerebral embolism occurs when a wandering blood clot (embolus) carried in the blood stream becomes lodged in one of the cerebral blood vessels.

The signs and symptoms of a stroke are as follows:

—The victim may be partially or totally unconscious.

—Respiration is slow with a snoring sound.

—Pupils are unequal in size.

—Paralysis or weakness on one side of the body or face is present.

—The victim loses the ability to speak, or the victim's speech is slurred.

The first aid care for a stroke victim is as follows:

- Maintain an open airway.

- Keep the tongue or saliva from blocking the air passage.

- Do not give the victim anything by mouth.

- Keep the victim lying down with head and shoulders raised to alleviate some of the pressure on the brain. If the victim is unconscious, place the victim on one side to allow fluids to drain.

- Do not move the victim any more than necessary.

- Keep the victim quiet and calm.

- Reassure the victim, who may be quite anxious or nervous.

- Administer oxygen, if available.

- Obtain medical care as soon as possible.

Foreign Bodies

Foreign Bodies in the Eye

Foreign bodies, such as particles of dirt, sand, cinders, coal dust, or fine pieces of metal, frequently are blown or driven into the eye and lodge there. They not only cause discomfort, but if not removed, can cause inflammation and possibly infection. Fortunately, through an increased flow of tears, nature dislodges many of these substances before any harm is done. In no case should the eye be rubbed, since rubbing may cause scratches of the delicate eye tissues or force a foreign particle with sharp edges into the tissues, making removal difficult. It is always much safer to send the person to a physician than for the first aider to attempt to remove foreign bodies.

The first aid care for a foreign body in the eye is as follows:

- The first maneuver should be to flush eye for 15 minutes with clean water, if available, holding the eyelids apart.

- Often a foreign body lodged under the upper eyelid can be removed by drawing the upper lid down over the lower lid; as the upper lid returns to its normal position, the undersurfaces will be drawn over the lashes of the lower lid and the foreign body removed by the wiping action of the eyelashes.

- A foreign body in the eye may also be removed by grasping the eyelashes of the upper lid and turning the lid over a cotton swab or similar object. The particle may then be carefully removed from the eyelid with the corner of a piece of sterile gauze (figure 10.02).

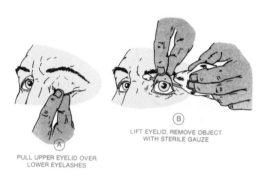

PULL UPPER EYELID OVER
LOWER EYELASHES

LIFT EYELID, REMOVE OBJECT
WITH STERILE GAUZE

FIGURE 10.02.—Removal of a foreign body in the eye.

- Particles lodged under the lower lid may be removed by pulling down the lower lid, exposing the inner surface. The corner of a piece of sterile gauze can be used to remove the foreign body.

Should a foreign body become lodged in the eyeball, do not attempt to disturb it, as it may be forced deeper into the eye and result in further damage. Place a bandage compress over both eyes. Take the victim to the doctor, because the removal of particles embedded in the eyeball requires skill.

Gentleness is essential in handling eye injuries. Never use the point of a knife blade, toothpick, sharpened match stick or any similar object to try to dislodge a foreign body in the eye.

If difficulty is experienced in removing a foreign body from the eye, send the victim to the doctor at once.

Foreign Bodies in the Nose

Foreign bodies in the nose usually can be removed without difficulty, but occasionally the services of a physician are required.

The first aid care for a foreign body in the nose is as follows:

- Sneezing induced by sniffing snuff or pepper, or tickling the opposite nostril with a feather usually will dislodge a foreign body in the nose.

- Do not blow the nose violently or with one nostril held shut.

Do not attempt to hook out the foreign body with a hairpin or similar object, because damage may be done to the tissues of the nasal cavity or the foreign body may be pushed into an inaccessible place.

Foreign Bodies in the Stomach

Foreign bodies such as pins, coins, nails and other objects are sometimes swallowed accidently. Except for pins, nails, or other sharp objects, swallowed foreign objects usually cause no great harm.

The first aid care for a foreign body in the stomach is as follows:

- Do not give anything to induce vomiting or bowel movement.

- Consult a physician immediately.

Foreign Bodies in the Ear

Small insects, pieces of rock, or other material may become lodged in the ear. Children sometimes put other objects, such as kernels of corn, peas, buttons or seeds in their ears. Such objects as seeds absorb moisture and swell in the ear, making dislodgement difficult and often causing painful inflammation.

The first aid care for foreign bodies in the ear is as follows:

- Do not insert pins, matchsticks, pieces of wire or other objects in the ear to dislodge foreign bodies because this may damage the tissue lining of the ear or perforate the ear drum.
- In the case of insects, turn the head to the side and put several drops of warm olive oil, mineral oil, or baby oil in the ear. Then let the oil run out and the drowned insect may come out.
- Consult a physician

Drugs

When drugs are administered under proper supervision, they can have positive effects in relieving pain and suffering, combating disease and saving lives. However, these same drugs can be deadly when abused and misused. For the purpose of this manual, drugs have been divided into four major categories:

—Narcotics
—Stimulants
—Depressants
—Hallucinogens

Narcotics are a class of drugs which induces sleep or stupor and relieves pain. They include opium, morphine, heroin, codeine, and methadone.

A stimulant is a substance which increases the reaction of the central nervous system. The most widely known and used stimulant is caffeine which is found in coffee, tea, cola, and other beverages. Amphetamines and cocaine are two other types of stimulants.

Depressants also affect the central nervous systems and are used to induce sleep or as mild sedatives or tranquilizers. Barbiturates fall into this category.

Hallucinogens are substances that produce hallucinations. These include marijuana, LSD, and mescaline.

First aid care for a drug overdose is as follows:

- Maintain an open airway and administer artifical ventilation or CPR, if indicated (see chapters 3 and 12).
- Treat for shock.
- Place an unconscious victim in a three-quarters prone position so that any secretions may drool from the mouth.
- Protect the person from injury
- It may be necessary to calm a person who has taken a hallucinogen. This person may need careful attention, reassurance, and protection from bodily harm or harming others.
- Get the victim to a physician or hospital as soon as possible. Any drug samples found around the victim should be taken to the hospital.

The following chart depicts commonly misused drugs, their methods of use, signs and symptoms associated with the drugs, their effects from overdose, and withdrawal symptoms.

COMMONLY USED DRUGS

	Drugs and slang terms	Method of use	Signs and symptoms	Effects of overdose	Withdrawal syndrome
NARCOTICS	Opium—"Pen Yan," "hop," "tar," "black stuff"	Oral, smoked	Scars (tracks) on the arm or back of hands. Pupils constricted & fixed. Scratches self frequently. Loss of appetite, frequently eats candy, cookies, and drinks sweet liquids. May have sniffles, red, watering eyes, and a cough which disappears when the user gets a "fix." Often leaves syringes, bent spoons, cotton, needles, metal bottle caps, etc., in locker or desk drawers. May be lethargic, drowsy and may go on the nod.	Slow and shallow breathing, clammy skin, convulsions, coma, possible death.	Watery eyes, runny nose, yawning, loss of appetite, irritability, tremors, panic, chills and sweating, cramps, nausea.
	Morphine—"white stuff," "hard stuff," "M," "morpho," "unkie," "Miss Emma"	Injected, oral			
	Heroin—"H", "junk," "Harry," "joy powder," "white stuff," "horse," "snow," "sugar," "smack"	Injected, oral			
	Codeine—"school boy"	Oral, injected			
	Methadone	Oral, injected			
DEPRESSANTS	Barbiturates—"goof ball," "goofers," "barbs"	Oral, injected	Slurred speech, disorientation, behavior like that of alcohol intoxication, but without the odor of alcohol on breath	Shallow respiration, cold and clammy skin, dilated pupils, weak and rapid pulse, coma possible death.	Anxiety, insomnia tremors, delirium, convulsions possible death.
	Chloral Hydrate—"Mickey Finn," "Mickey," "Peter," "knockout drops"	Oral			
	Tranquilizers	Oral			
	Other depressants	Oral			
STIMULANTS	Amphetamines—"bennies," "pep pills," "peaches," "roses," "heart," "cart wheels," "dexies," "oranges," "football"	Oral, injected	Increased alertness, excitement, euphoria, dilated pupils, increased pulse rate and blood pressure, insomnia, loss of appetite.	Agitation, increase in body temperature, hallucinations, convulsions, possible death.	Apathy, long periods of sleep, irritability, depression disorientation.
	Cocaine—"coke," "snow," "happy dust," "C," "flake," "speedballs," "snowbirds," "Cecil," "stardust," "Bernice gold dust"	Sniffed, injected			
HALLUCINOGENS	Other Stimulants	Oral			
	LSD—"acid," "cubes," "sugar," "25," "the big D"	Oral	Illusions and hallucinations, poor perception of time and distance.	Longer, more intense "trip" episodes, psychosis, possible death.	None
	Mescaline—"peyote," "plants," "buttons"	Oral, injected			
	Other Hallucinogens	Oral, injected, sniffed	Euphoria, relaxed inhibitions, increased appetite, disoriented behavior.	Fatigue, paranoia, possible psychosis.	Insomnia, hyperactivity and decreased appetite reported in a limited number of individuals.
	Marihuana—"pot," "tea," "grass," "weed," "stuff," "hay," "joints," "Mary Jane," "reefers," Acapulco Gold"	Oral			
	Hashish	Smoked			

CHAPTER 11. POISONS

Poisons are any substances which act to produce harmful effects on the normal body processes. There are numerous ways in which these substances may enter the body (figure 11.01):

—Ingestion (mouth).

—Inhalation in the form of noxious dusts, gases, fumes or mists.

—Injection into the body tissues or blood stream by hypodermic needles or the bites of poisonous snakes, insects or rabid animals.

—Absorption through the skin (mercury or certain other poisonous liquids) or contact by the skin (poisonous plants and certain fungi).

FIGURE 11.01.—Causes of poisoning.

Poisoning by Ingestion (Mouth)

The chief causes of poisoning by ingestion are as follows:

—Overdose of medicine (intentional or accidental).

—Medicines, household cleaners and chemicals, within the reach of children.

—Combining drugs and alcohol.

—Poisons transferred from the original container to food container.

—Carelessness on the part of those who should know better.

The signs and symptoms of poisoning by ingestion are as follows:

—Nausea, vomiting, and diarrhea.

—Severe abdominal pain and cramps.

—Slowed respiration and circulation.

—Corrosive poisons (strong acids and alkalis) may corrode, burn, or destroy the tissues of the mouth, throat and stomach.

—Contents of a drug bottle spilled out, and not all of the contents accounted for.

—Liquids such as kerosene or turpentine may leave characteristic odors on the breath.

—Certain poisons may stain the mouth.

The following is first aid care for poisoning by ingestion:

• Dilute the substance by giving the victim milk or water.

• Call the nearest control center. This can be done more quickly than transporting the victim to the hospital.

• In most cases, if medical help is not available try to remove the substance from the stomach before it is absorbed by the system. This gives the victim a better chance of recovery.

- Vomiting should not be induced in the following cases:

  —When the victim has swallowed a strong acid or alkali which would cause further damage when coming back up. In such cases, the victim should be given a glass of milk or water and monitored for breathing difficulties.

  —If a petroleum product has been swallowed, because it can cause a form of pneumonia if inhaled into the lungs.

  —When the victim is unconscious or semi-conscious because the victim might suck vomitus into the lung.

  —When the victim goes into convulsions or has convulsed.

  —If the victim has a serious heart problem.

Check with the nearest poison control center to find out the best method to induce vomiting. The victim would be sitting and leaning forward to prevent vomitus from going into the lungs. Collect the vomitus and take it to the hospital.

- The poison container should be taken to the hospital along with the victim.

Poisoning by Inhalation

Certain toxic or noxious gases may stop respiration by a direct poisoning effect or by preventing the transport of oxygen by the red blood cells. Such gases are encountered in mining, oil drilling, and similar industries. They include sulfur dioxide, the oxides of nitrogen, ammonia, hydrogen sulfide, hydrogen cyanide, and carbon monoxide.

The signs and symptoms of inhaled poisons are as follows:

  —Shortness of breath.

  —Coughing.

  —Cyanosis (bluish color).

To provide first aid care for poisoning by inhalation, proceed as follows:

- Remove the victim to fresh air as quickly as possible. The rescuer should not risk entering a hazardous atmosphere without proper personal protective equipment.

- In appropriate cases, initiate artificial ventilation or cardiopulmonary resuscitation (see chapters 3 and 12).

- If the victim is breathing, administer oxygen if available.

- Treat the victim for shock.

Carbon Monoxide

Carbon monoxide, a product of incomplete combustion, is probably the most common of the poisonous gases. Overexposure can prove fatal. Carbon monoxide causes asphyxia because it combines with the hemoglobin of the blood much more readily than oxygen does. The blood, therefore, carries less and less oxygen from the lungs to the body tissues. The first symptoms of asphyxia appear when a 30 percent blood saturation level has been reached.

The signs and symptoms of carbon monoxide are as follows:

—Headache.

—Dizziness.

—Yawning.

—Faintness.

—Lethargy and stupor.

—Mucous membranes becoming bright cherry red in color.

—Lips and earlobes possibly turning bluish in color.

—Nausea or vomiting.

To provide first aid care for carbon monoxide poisoning, proceed as follows:

- Take the victim to fresh air.

- Maintain an open airway.

- Perform artificial ventilation, if required.

- Administer oxygen if available.

Poisons Injected Into the Skin

Poisons can enter the skin by means of injections or bites of animals, poisonous snakes, and insects. Nonpoisonous insects and drugs can be poisonous to some people. An allergic reaction to a nonpoisonous insect bite or drug results in anaphylactic shock.

First aid care is aimed at minimizing the travel of the poison to the heart. The general first aid care for poisons injected into the skin is as follows:

- Keep the person calm, quiet, and at rest.

- All jewelry, bracelets, rings, watches, etc., should be removed from the bitten extremity, in case of swelling.

- Apply a constricting bandage above and below the bite at the edge of the swelling, loosely enough to slide a finger under the bandage.

- The pulse should be checked periodically below the bite; bandages are only to be used as a constriction, not as a tourniquet.

- Transport the victim to a medical facility as quickly as possible while monitoring for changes in respiration and circulation.

Bites of Animals

Any warm-blooded animal may suffer from rabies. If a person is bitten by an animal, always suspect the animal to be rabid until it is proved otherwise. The saliva from a rabid animal enters the wound caused by the bite, transmitting the disease to the victim. If possible the animal should be captured or identified and held for medical observation. First aid care for animal bites is as follows:

- Wash the wound with soap and water and rinse well.

- Take the victim to a medical facility as quickly as possible.

Snakebites

Coral snakes, copperheads, rattlesnakes, and water moccasins are the four types of poisonous snakes in the United States (figure 11.02).

FIGURE 11.02.—Poisonous snakes.

The signs and symptoms of a snakebite are as follows:

—A sharp, stinging pain with one or more puncture marks in the area.

—There may be swelling and discoloration, and the bitten area is painful.

—As the poison goes through the body, other symptoms develop; weakness, nausea and vomiting, weak and rapid pulse, shock and respiratory distress (figure 11.03).

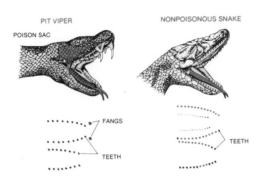

FIGURE 11.03.—Snakebites.

The first aid care for snakebites is as follows:

- Start care at once.

- Keep the person lying down and quiet with the injured part immobile and lower than the rest of the body.

- Remove all rings, watches, and bracelets from the extremities.

- Apply cold packs to wound, if available.

- Apply constricting bands above and below the area. The constricting bands should be tight enough to slow down surface circulation but not so tight as to cut off arterial blood.

- If medical help will not be available within an hour, incisions might be made within the first 20 minutes. Make an incision, no more than ⅛ inch deep and no more than ½ inch long lengthwise through the fang marks. Press around cut to make it bleed, or suction it. Do not make incisions if the bite is near a major vessel. It should be noted that there are problems with this procedure. If the incision is too deep, it may damage underlying tissues; if it is too shallow, it may not penetrate the venom pool.

- If swelling continues past the constricting bands, put on another past the swelling and loosen the first band.
- Treat the victim for shock. Do not give any stimulants or alcohol.
- Identify the snake if possible. If the snake can be killed, take it to the hospital with the victim.
- For persons who frequent regions infested with poisonous snakes, it is recommended that a snakebite kit be carried.

Insect Bites and Stings

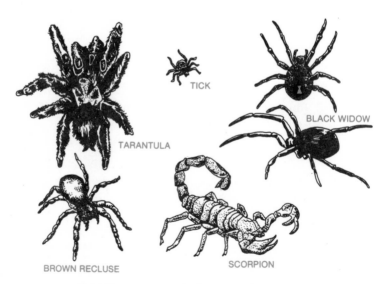

TICK

BLACK WIDOW

TARANTULA

BROWN RECLUSE

SCORPION

FIGURE 11.04.—Poisonous insects.

194

Many insects bite or sting, but few can cause serious symptoms by themselves, unless of course, the person is allergic to them. However, some insects transmit diseases. For example, certain types of mosquitoes transmit malaria, yellow fever, and other diseases; certain types of ticks transmit spotted or Rocky Mountain fever; and certain types of biting flies transmit tularemia or rabbit fever.

Occasionally, stinging or biting insects that have been feeding on or have been in contact with poisonous substances, can transmit this poison at the time of the sting or bite.

Persons who have experienced serious reactions from previous insect bites should be urged to secure any possible immunization or have an antidote readily available to prevent more serious results from future insect bites and stings.

The signs and symptoms of insect bites and stings are as follows:

—The stings of bees, wasps, yellowjackets, and hornets, and the bites of mosquitoes, ticks, fleas, and bedbugs usually cause only local irritation and pain in the region stung or bitten.

—Moderate swelling and redness may occur and some itching, burning and pain may be present.

The first aid care for insect bites and stings is as follows:

• The sting area should be inspected to determine whether the stinger is still left in the body. If it is, remove it in order to prevent further injection of toxin. The stinger should be carefully scraped off the skin rather than grasped with tweezers because this might squeeze toxin into the body.

• Application of ice or ice water to the bite helps to slow absorption of toxin into the blood stream. A paste of baking soda and water can also be applied to the bite.

• The victim should be observed for signs of an allergic reaction. For people who are allergic, use a constricting bandage. If the sting is on an extremity, use ice, maintain an open airway, treat for shock, and get the allergic victim to medical help as quickly as possible.

Bites and Stings of Spiders, Centipedes, Tarantulas, and Scorpions

The effect of stings and bites of spiders, centipedes, tarantulas, and scorpions in some instances are much more severe than those of the insects previously mentioned. They may cause alarming symptoms.

The signs and symtpoms of these bites are as follows:

—Generally, the bite consists of two small pinpoint punctures of the skin and produce local swelling and redness with a smarting, burning pain.

—Prostration, sweating, and nausea may appear.

—Pain or cramping in the back, shoulders, chest, and limbs may develop.

—In some instances the symptoms are mild and subside within 6 to 12 hours, but occasionally they are severe and cause a state of collapse.

The black widow is a moderately large, glossy black spider with very fine hairs over the body giving it a silky appearance. On the underside of the abdomen is a characteristic red or crimson marking in the form of an hourglass. Only the female is poisonous, the male, which is smaller, is harmless.

The brown recluse spider bite injects a venom which causes a limited destruction of red blood cells and certain other blood changes. The victim may develop chills, fever, joint pains, nausea, and vomiting. A generalized rash may also develop within 24 to 48 hours.

Most species of scorpions in this country do not inject a toxin generally harmful to humans. The sting may result in local swelling and discoloration, similar to wasp sting, and may sometimes cause allergic reactions. The sting of the more dangerous species of scorpions causes little or no swelling or discoloration, but locally there will be a tingling or burning sensation. Considerable discomfort may ensue. Death, although unlikely, occurs occasionally in infants and young children and might conceivably occur in older persons. The poison acts mainly on the nervous system.

Tarantulas are hairy spiders. Those found in the southwestern United States are harmless, but occasionally a victim will have an allergic reaction to the injected venom. Tarantulas coming into the country in imported fruit may be more poisonous. Their bites may cause marked pain and local redness with swelling. Death is extremely rare. The first aid care is as follows:

- Where the bites and stings produce little or no pain, and swelling and discoloration do not occur, treat as for the less poisonous bites or stings of insects.

- Where the swelling and pain are rapid and severe, treat as for poisonous snake bites. Put a cold pack over the area.

- Get the person to medical help as quickly as possible.

- Keep the victim lying down and quiet to retard absorption of the poison into the circulatory system.

Poisoning by Contact With Skin

Dermatoses

Many substances in the form of gases, fumes, mists, liquids, and dusts, cause poisoning or dermatoses when they come in contact with the skin. Dermatoses are diseases of the skin and its underlying tissue (hair follicles, oil glands, and sweat glands). These diseases change the normal structure of the skin and produce irritation and inflammation. Usually, dermatoses do not progress rapidly, but show themselves gradually after continued exposure to the cause. Persons who note changes in the normal texture of their skin or continued irritation of the skin should seek medical advice before a chronic dermatoses develops. Needless discomfort and loss of time can be prevented by early medical care.

The first aid care for the victim of contact poisoning is as follows:

- Remove contaminated clothing and flood the area with plenty of water.

- If the poison has contacted the eyes, wash with plenty of water.

- Watch the person for signs of shock and changes in respiration.

Poison ivy, Poison oak, and Poison Sumac Poisoning

These poisonous plants grow as vines or shrubs, waist to shoulder high. The poison comes mainly from their leaves but also may be from bruising their roots, stems, and berries. The smoke from burning brush containing these plants has been known to carry the poisons considerable distances.

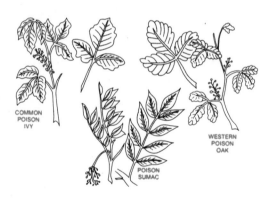

COMMON POISON IVY

WESTERN POISON OAK

POISON SUMAC

FIGURE 11.05.—Poisonous plants.

The signs and symptoms of this kind of skin poisoning are as follows:

—There is a red rash, with some swelling, itching, and burning, followed by formation of blisters of various sizes filled with blood serum. The symptoms appear on the exposed skin surfaces, usually the hands, wrists, and arms, six hours to several days after exposure.

—The blisters may fill with pus or contaminated fluid. When they break, crusts and scabs are formed. Considerable fluid may exude from broken blisters.

—When the affected area is considerable and the inflammation is severe, there may be fever, headache, and general body weakness.

The first aid care for the victim of such poisoning is as follows:

- Contaminated clothing and jewelry should be removed.

- Wash the area with soap and water.

- A calamine preparation or a soothing skin lotion can be used if the rash is mild.

- If a severe reaction appears, seek medical help.

CHAPTER 12. CARDIOPULMONARY RESUSCITATION

Cardiopulmonary resuscitation (CPR) involves the use of artificial ventilation (mouth-to-mouth breathing) and external heart compression (rhythmic pressure on the breastbone). These techniques can only be learned through training and supervised practice. Incorrect application of external heart compressions may result in complications such as damage to internal organs, fracture of ribs or sternum, or separation of cartilage from ribs. (Rib fractures may occur when compressions are being correctly performed but this is not an indication to stop compression.) Application of cardiopulmonary resuscitation when not required could result in cardiac arrest. It should be emphasized that when CPR is *properly applied,* the likelihood of complications is minimal and acceptable in comparison with the alternative—death.

Sudden Death

Sudden death is the immediate and unexpected cessation of respiration and functional circulation. The term "sudden death" is synonymous with cardiopulmonary arrest or heart lung arrest. In the definition, the phrase "sudden and unexpected" is extremely important. A person who dies gradually of an organic disease such as cancer, or is under treatment for a chronic heart condition and has gradual but progressive loss of heart function, cannot be correctly classified as "sudden death." Cardiac arrest, when the heart stops pumping blood, may occur suddenly and unexpectedly in younger, healthy people for any one of the number of reasons:

—Heart attack.

—Electric shock.

—Asphyxiation.

—Suffocation.

—Drowning.

—Allergic reaction.

—Choking.

—Secondary to severe injury.

The moment the heart stops beating and breathing ceases, the person is considered clinically dead. However, the vital centers of the central nervous system within the brain may remain viable for four to six minutes more. Indeed much of the body remains "biologically alive" for much longer. The tissue most sensitive to oxygen deprivation is the brain. Irreversible death probably begins to occur to human brain cells somewhere between four and six minutes after oxygen has been excluded. This condition is referred to as biological death. Resuscitation in the treatment of sudden death depends upon this grace period of four to six minutes. After that period, even though the heart might yet be restarted, the chance of return to a normal functional existence is lessened. In sudden death, CPR should be started even though the four-to-six-minute mark has been passed, but the urgency of re-establishing the oxygenation system of the body, that is, ventilation and circulation, within this four- to six-minute grace period cannot be overemphasized.

Heart Attacks

Diseases of the heart and blood vessels are the leading cause of death in the United States. Over 650,000 people die annually from heart attacks. Of these, approximately 350,000 die outside the hospital within the first two hours of the arrest.

Recognition of the early warning signs is extremely important. The following are the early warning signs of an impending heart attack:

—Uncomfortable pressure, squeezing, fullness, or dull pain in the center of the chest.

—Pain may radiate into the shoulders, arm, neck or jaws.

—Sweating.

—Nausea.

—Shortness of breath.

—Feeling of weakness.

—Pale and sick look.

A person need not exhibit all these symptoms to have a heart attack. The symptoms of a heart attack may come and go. Also, quite often the victim attributes these symptoms to another cause such as indigestion.

Risk Factors

Certain factors that have been identified as increasing an individual's risk of some form of cardiovascular disease. Some factors a person has no control over. These include heredity, sex, race, and age. However, people can do a tremendous amount to improve their physical condition and reduce the chance of cardiovascular disease. Every person should take the following precautions:

- Have regular medical checkups.

- Follow doctor's advice on controlling high blood pressure.

- Do not smoke.

- Eat a balanced diet, low in saturated fat and cholestrol.

- If overweight, reduce.

- Avoid stress; alter one's life style if necessary.

- Get regular physical exercise.

Recognize the Problem

The person who initiates emergency heart-lung resuscitation has two responsibilities:

— to apply emergency measures to prevent irreversible changes to the vital centers of the body.

— To be sure the victim receives definitive medical care; this requires hospitalization.

When sudden death occurs, the rescuer must act immediately upon recognition of heart failure. In order to prevent biological death, the rescuer must be able to do the following:

— Recognize rapidly the apparent stoppage of heart action and respiration.

— Provide artificial ventilation to the lungs.

— Provide artificial circulation of the blood.

In addition to performing CPR, the rescuer must summon help in order that an ambulance and/or a physician may be called to the scene.

CPR Procedure

The CPR procedures should be learned and practiced on a training manikin under the guidance of a qualified instructor. The step by step procedure for cardiopulmonary resuscitation is as follows:

• Establish unresponsiveness. Shake the victim's shoulder and shout, "Are you O.K.?" The individual's response will indicate to the rescuer if the victim is just sleeping or if he/she is unconscious (figure 12.01).

FIGURE 12.01.—Recognition of the problem.

- Call for help. The rescuer will need help, either to assist in performing CPR or to call for medical help.

- Position the victim. If the victim found in a crumpled up and face down, the rescuer must roll the victim over; this is done while calling for help (figure 12.02).

FIGURE 12.02.—Turning the victim.

- When rolling the victim over, care must be taken that broken bones are not further complicated by improper handling. The victim is rolled as a unit so that the head and shoulders move simultaneously with no twisting.

- Kneel beside the victim, a few inches to the side.

- The arm nearest the rescuer should be raised above the victim's head.

- The victim's legs should be as straight as possible.

- The rescuer's hand closest to the victim's head should be placed on the victim's head and neck to prevent them from twisting.

- The rescuer should use his other hand to grasp under the victim's arm furthest from him. This will be the point at which the rescuer exerts the pull in rolling the body over.

- Pull carefully under the arm, and the hips and torso will follow the shoulders with minimal twisting.

- Be sure to watch the neck and keep it in line with the rest of the body.

- The victim should now be flat on his or her back.

- Open the airway. The most common cause of airway obstruction in an unconscious victim is the tongue. The tongue is attached to the lower jaw; moving the jaw forward, lifts the tongue away from the back of the throat and opens the airway.

  - Kneel at the victirn's side with knee nearest the head opposite the victim's shoulders.

  - Place one hand under the neck and lift the other hand is placed on the victim's forehead and pushed downward to tilt the head (figure 12.03).

FIGURE 12.03.—Positioning the head and neck.

- Establish breathlessness. The airway must be open to determine breathlessness.

  - Turn your head toward the victim's feet with your cheek ear close over the victim's mouth.

  - *Look* for a rise and fall in the victim's chest.

  - *Listen* for air exchange at the mouth and nose.

  - *Feel* for the flow of air (figure 12.04).

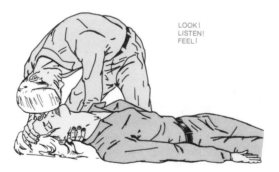

LOOK!
LISTEN!
FEEL!

FIGURE 12.04.—Establishing breathlessness.

- Watch for signs of cyanosis: bluish or grayish color in the lips, tongue, ear lobes, nailbeds, and skin due to deficiency of oxygen in the blood.

Sometimes opening and maintaining an open airway is all that is necessary to restore breathing.

- Provide artificial ventilation.

  - If the victim is not breathing give four quick breaths by mouth-to-mouth or mouth-to-nose ventilation (figure 12.05).

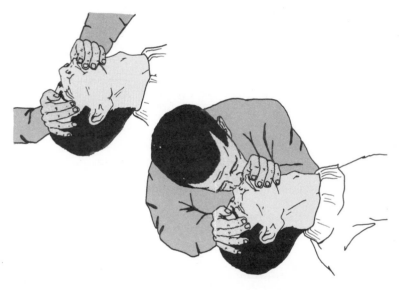

FIGURE 12.05.—Four quick breaths.

  - Do not allow for lung deflation between each of the four ventilations.

- Check for pulse. The rescuer must check the victim for a pulse to determine whether external cardiac compressions are necessary.

  - Maintain an open airway position by holding the forehead of the victim.

- The rescuer's fingertips are placed on the victim's windpipe by sliding the fingertips in the groove of the neck nearest the rescuer and pressing gently (figure 12.06).

- Check the victim's pulse for at least five seconds but no more than ten seconds.

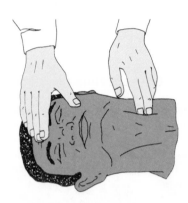

FIGURE 12.06.—Checking the pulse.

- If a pulse is present, continue administering artificial ventilation once every 5 seconds or 12 times a minute. If not, make arrangements to send for trained medical assistance and begin CPR.

- Perform cardiac compressions.

  - When performing external cardiac compressions, the victim should be in a horizontal position, on a hard, flat surface.

  - The rescuer should locate the bottom of the rib cage and run the fingers up to or in the notch where the ribs meet the sternum (breastbone) (figure 12.07).

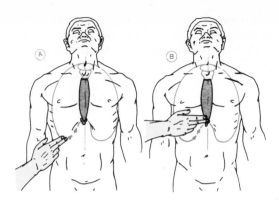

FIGURE 12.07.—Locating the xiphoid process.

- The ring finger is placed on the notch with the middle and index fingers resting on the sternum.

- The heel of the other hand is placed on the sternum next to the fingers in the notch in the rib cage (A of figure 12.08).

- The hand used to locate the notch at the rib cage is then placed on top and parallel to the hand which is on the sternum.

- The fingers must be kept off the chest, by either interlocking or extending them (B and C of figure 12.08).

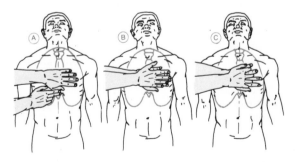

FIGURE 12.08.—Correct hand position on the sternum.

- Elbows are kept straight by locking them.

- The shoulders of the rescuer are brought directly over the hands so that pressure is exerted straight downward (figure 12.09).

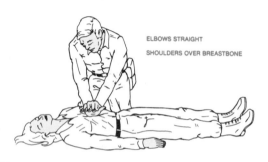

ELBOWS STRAIGHT

SHOULDERS OVER BREASTBONE

FIGURE 12.09.—Exerting pressure downward.

- Exert enough downward pressure to depress the sternum of an adult 1½ to 2 inches.

- Each compression should squeeze the heart between the sternum and spine to pump blood through the body.

- The rescuer must then totally release pressure in order to allow the heart to refill completely with blood.

- The heel of the rescuer's hand should remain in contact with the victim's chest at all times (figure 12.10).

- Compressions should be down and up in a smooth manner.

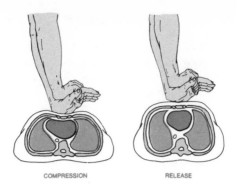

COMPRESSION   RELEASE

FIGURE 12.10.—Cardiac compressions.

Single Rescuer CPR

- Perform 15 cardiac compressions at a rate of 80 per minute, counting "one and two and three and . . . . fifteen."

- Move to the head, tilt it, and give two quick full breaths (artificial ventilation.)

- Move back to the chest, locate the hand position and give 15 compressions at a rate of 80 per minute.

- Repeat this cycle four times.

- After the second cycle, look, listen and feel for breathing. Also check the carotid pulse in the neck for a heartbeat for no more than five seconds.

- If breathing and heartbeat are absent, resume CPR.

- Stop and check for heartbeat and respiration every four to five minutes thereafter.

- Never interrupt CPR for more than five seconds.

Two-Rescuer CPR

The second rescuer to arrive on the scene should tell the first rescuer he or she is qualified and willing to help. The second rescuer is positioned at the head on the opposite side from the first rescuer. The second rescuer will then check the victim's pulse while the first rescuer is still compressing the chest. After a couple of seconds the second rescuer says "Stop compressions." The first rescuer stops compressions for 5 seconds so the second rescuer can check for the victim's pulse. If no pulse is found, two-rescuer CPR is begun. The first rescuer reduces the compression rate from 80 to 60 compressions per minute, counting "one-one thousand, two-one thousand, ... five-one thousand." The rescue breathing is done delivering a single breath during the upstroke of every fifth compression. The rescuer giving the compressions should count out loud so the other rescuer knows when to ventilate.

Changing Positions—Two Rescuers

- The rescuer performing the compressions gives the command, "Change — after — the — next — breath," instead of counting.

- After giving a breath, the rescuer performing rescue breathing moves to the victim's chest and locates the proper hand position by finding the notch where the ribs meet the sternum.

- Following the third chest compression, the rescuer that is to take over chest compressions slides the hand in place, pushing the other rescuer's hand out of the way.

- The rescuer that has been taken over the chest compressions positions his body and hands and continues with the fourth and fifth compressions.

- The other rescuer is positioned to ventilate after the fifth compression.

Infant Resuscitation

For infant resuscitation proceed as follows:

- Establish unresponsiveness by the shake and shout method.

- Open the airway, taking care not to overextend the neck.

- Establish breathlessness.

- Puff cheeks, using the air in the mouth to give four quick ventilations.

- Pulselessness may be determined by checking the carotid pulse or the precordial pulse. To locate the precordial pulse, place two fingers over the left nipple.

- If heartbeat is absent, begin CPR at once:

  - Place two fingers over the midportion of the sternum.

  - Compress at the rate of 80 to 100 times per minute.

  - Sternum displacement should be from ½ to ¾ of an inch.

  - Ventilate after every five compressions.

Gastric Distention

One problem that may occur during artificial ventilation is the accumulation of air in the victim's stomach. Air in the stomach can result in two problems:

—Reduction in the volume of air that enters the lungs because the diaphragm is farther forward than normal.

—Vomiting.

If there is a marked distention in the victim's stomach, the condition should be corrected. To reduce distention, proceed as follows:

- Turn the victim on his or her side.

- Using the flat of the hand, the rescuer should gently press on the victim's abdomen to force air from the stomach. The point of pressure should be between the victim's rib cage and navel.

- Clear the mouth and continue resuscitation.

Transportation of the Victim

Never move the victim until the victim is in stable condition ready for transportation. Uninterrupted CPR should be performed during transportation. The only possible exception would be when moving the victim up or down a stairway. If the victim is to be moved up or down stairs, CPR should be given at the head and foot of the stairs. Under no circumstances should CPR be interrupted for more than 15 seconds.

Termination of CPR

Under normal circumstances CPR may be terminated under four conditions:

- The victim is revived.
- A person with more training than the rescuer arrives at the scene of the emergency and takes over.
- The person performing CPR becomes exhausted.
- A doctor pronounces the victim dead.

BIBLIOGRAPHY

American Academy of Orthopaedic Surgeons. Emergency Care and Transportation of the Sick and Injures. George Banta Co., Menasha, Wis., 1977, 293 pp.

American College of Surgeons. Early Care of the Injured Patient. W.B. Saunders Company, Philadelphia, Pa., 1976, 436 pp.

American Heart Association. Standards for Cardiopulmonary Resuscitation (CPR) and Emergency Cardiac Care (ECC). American Heart Association, New York, 1973, 35 pp.

American National Red Cross. Standard First Aid and Personal Safety. Doubleday and Company, Inc., Garden City, N.Y., 1973, 268 pp.

Byers, Linda and Marilyn Hutchinson. First Aid. Safety Manual No. 3, Mining Enforcement and Safety Administration, 1976, 66 pp.

Grant, Harvey and Robert Murray. Emergency Care. Robert J. Brady Co., Bowie, Md., 1978, 538 pp.

Henderson, John. Emergency Medical Guide. McGraw-Hill Book Company, New York, 1973, 637 pp.

Kelly, John S. (rev. by). First Aid for the Mineral and Allied Industries. BuMines Handbook, 1971, 195 pp.

Ohio Trade and Industrial Education Service. Emergency Victim Care. Columbus, Ohio, State Department of Education, 1971, 353 pp.

U.S. Bureau of Mines. First Aid Instruction Course. 1970, 184 pp.

INDEX

A

PAGE

B

C

I

J

K

L